Play, illusion, Reality, and Trauma

Play, Illusion, Reality, and Trauma

What Can a Psychoanalyst Learn from Charlie Chaplin?

Albert J. Brok, PhD

IPBOOKS.net
International Psychoanalytic Books

International Psychoanalytic Books (IPBooks)
New York • IPBooks.net

Published by IPBooks, Queens, NY
Online at: www.IPBooks.net

ISBN: 978-1-949093-52-0

Table of Contents

About the Author

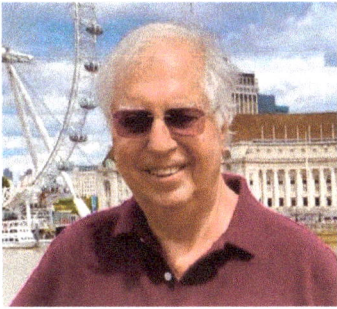

Albert Brok, PhD, CGP: Dr. Brok is the Director of Group and Couple Therapy and training analyst at TIMH. He is on the Board of the Division of Psychoanalysis, American Psychological Association and Past President of Section I , and Chair Film and International Committee. He serves on the Postgraduate Faculty of Adelphi University and is a member of the commission on film, and the commission for the study of technology and subjectivity, Argentine Psychoanalytic Association, Buenos Aires, as well as Guest Lecturer Asociación Psicoanalítica de Madrid. Dr Brok has co-authored five books , and over 100 articles across a wide variety of topics ranging from Psychoanalysis, Analytic Group Therapy, Cinema, Couples Therapy, and Aging. Being Bilingual, he has published numerous articles in English and Spanish. Some of his recent publications include, The Lost Father and Regressive Desire in Almodovar's "Talk to Her", in A. Kramer-Richards and Lucille Spira (Edts), Pedro Almodovar: A Cinema of Desire, Passion and Compulsion, IP Books, NY 2018, Psychodynamic Couples Counseling, in, Behavioral, Humanistic-Existential and Psychodynamic Approaches to Couples Counseling, 2017) (M Reiter and R. Chenaill)

editors;. La busqueda ambivalente del Padre Perdido, Journal de Ética y Cine, Vol 9, (2), 2019, Buenos Aires;) and Hope, Envy, Illusion and Reality, in Analytic Group Therapy, Group, 2013. 37 (3). His, pioneering book co-authored with J. Caligor, and N. Fieldsteel, Individual and Group Therapy, Combining Analytic Treatments., Basic Books, 1984 ,has been republished a number of times and has won the Postgraduate Center Award, for significance to the field. He is former Associate professor and Chair of Clinical Psychology, New School for Social Research, and Professor of Education and Supervisor of Clinical Psychology. TC Columbia University. He is in private practice in New York City.

Acknowledgments

A lot goes into writing a book, long or short. This particular treatise, is a creative enterprise that has percolated in my thoughts for quite some time. Way back in fact to when my father would take me to see Chaplin's silent films in an Art House in Buenos Aires, where we lived from my ages 4 - 12. Later my parents would talk about Chaplin's later films, kindling my interest in his work and the political situation of the times. An interest I continued as a young adult in New York while in Graduate School. Things lay fallow for some years after, and then as I trained in Psychoanalysis, and Analytic Group Therapy, I for whatever reasons, put together in my mind some of the issues in Charlie's career, with the sense of the complexity and very special capacity needed to be both an *involved witness*, and audience with my patients. And, on some occasions how humor and play would either be inappropriate or appropriate given the idiosyncratic circumstances of a given session, which of course is embedded in the context of previous sessions, as well as the particular history of both my patient and myself. Complex issues that are most well illustrated, I believe in Chaplin's later talking films where play/humor became intertwined with politics/reality and trauma in a difficult paradox for some audiences to negotiate. A dividing line in his career.

Just why I revived all these memories about Chaplin when I did in my middle years are not clear; most likely, I was recapturing and honoring all those good discussions and moments with my playful , creative, warm father who simultaneously had a balanced awareness of how serious things were in this world, Benjamin Brok, my dad, was an important part of a familial and friendship culture my parents were part of that valued discussion and creative thought. In that light, it is a book written in his memory, a wonderfully flexible man in so many ways, who let me stand on his shoulders to see far and wide.

Intertwined with all this history, was the beginning of a series of lovely Invitations to present on various aspects of the themes in this book, at the Oklahoma Psychoanalytic Society, the Tampa Bay Institute for Psychanalytic Studies, the American Psychological Association programs of Division 39 in Chicago and New Orleans, The Argentine Psychoanalytic Association, as well as presentations at local Institutes in New York .- For me this was wonderful as it helped me refine and hone my ideas both theoretical and clinical about play, humor, reality , Illusion and trauma. Many learned and creative colleagues were discussants in these presentations. These include, Isaac Tylim, PsyD, K .William Fried, PhD, of New York, Nestor Goldstein, MD and Federico Aberastury, MD of the Argentine Psychoanalytic Association in Buenos Aires, and Mary Beth Cresci, PhD. Post Doctoral Program, Adelphi University, Vincenzo Conigliaro, MD of the Training institute for Mental Health, Lycia Alexander-Guerra, MD of the Tampa Bay Institute for Psychoanalytic Studies, just to name a few.

In the mix of all this was so much I learned and formulated by my exposure to many sharp minds as a young Professor at TC Columbia

University as well as my time teaching at The Graduate Faculty of The New School for Social Research, The Postgraduate Center for Mental Health and TIMH. Locations where I produced other writings that lent adjunctive ideas that would end up in this book. How fortunate to do the work I do where I learn from patients and they from me. To ensure anonymity, the clinical vignettes herein are disguised composites of work with various cases, mine and those of colleagues over many years. The material is offered not as evidence, but for the purpose of illustrating the theoretical concepts involved and what they look like when applied to actual clinical material.

Finally, I give special thanks for the steadfast support of Ellen Gussaroff, PhD, my partner, who helped me through my later years to keep my spark and motivation to complete this and many other ventures. So I trust you will enjoy, critique and think about my creative offering.

CHAPTER 1

Introduction

This work presents some thoughts on Play, Illusion, Reality, and Trauma in relation to the process between patient and analyst. A creative part of our journey of discussion includes a look at the long career of Charlie Chaplin, in terms of his relationship with his audience as a metaphor for the analyst as audience to his patient and vice versa.

Patient and analyst, audience and artist, are mutually and hopefully salubriously intertwined as "involved witnesses" with each other's communication, be they verbal or non-verbal. The level at which these communications are reacted to, the attributions made about them, the connectiveness created, and the therapeutic value derived in the case of analysis, depends on many idiosyncratic factors, both external and internal to the participants involved. I will provide some examples of these factors, both clinical and artistic, from individual and group therapy in later chapters of this work. In the process, I will define and elaborate the clinical relevancy of play and the concept of a "Playing Alliance" vs "Working Alliance," as well as the irrelevancy of play at certain moments therapeutically. I will also discuss the idea of an aesthetic therapeutic contract and the differentiation of enactments from what I have come to term "actments," (Brok 2014, 2016), as well as the paradox of reality and illusion and the impact of trauma in human experience.

A Note on Chaplin

Charlie Chaplin had a remarkably long career in motion pictures, spanning some 53 years. His delayed transition from silent to talking pictures is directly correlated with a shift in themes in his later work. As Chaplin found his cinema voice, his films moved from the world of illusion, play, humor, and poignancy to the more overtly rational/serious world of political/ social messages, focused/satire and existential/developmental dilemmas. Nevertheless, he still attempted to retain play and humor in his film narrative. We shall see how this attempt led to the loss of some of his audience, that I suggest is similar to the difficulty some analysts might have in maintaining a connection with their patients who relate playfully and humorously, either inappropriately, or in a potentially appropriate spontaneous way that activates particular conflictual anxiety for the analyst and/or, when the analyst who may be overly comfortable with seriousness, and analyzing, cannot access an important playful way of being from his repertoire. *Simply put, what may be funny or playful for one person may not be for another as a function of that other's life experience.* I will suggest that Chaplin lost some of his audience by trying to keep inserting humor and play into serious topics that hurt too much, and whose paradoxical element were difficult for some to digest. The acceptance of paradox is an important human capacity, without it we see things as too one-sided; however, when used to communicate a message, it has its limits for some audiences. Analogous examples from clinical work will be presented in subsequent chapters.[1]

I will also suggest that Chaplin used cinema as a metaphoric "dream screen" and his film audience as important witnesses, much as a patient uses his analyst as audience and involved witness to his dreams, both for personal awareness/development, and as a container for projections and the desire for feedback/interpretation. In the clinical situation, this is an example of what I term, "dual montage" (Brok 2014).

Finally, as indicated above, I will introduce the concept of an "aesthetic therapeutic contract" between patient and analyst, as similar to that of artist and audience, and compare the tendency of film audiences to sometimes understand and sometimes misinterpret an artist's message at particular points in cultural–political history. I compare this with the analyst's ability to be an involved witness and experientially empathic audience to his patient's productions at certain times, while at other times being subject to blockage or countertransference as a function of the analyst's cultural/historical/traumatic experience. Under the latter conditions, the "aesthetic quality" of the relationship may be lost.

---

1 Also, I believe there is a fine but discernable line between paradoxical comedy/ humor in light of tragic experience that is different from comic relief. We can see this in Chaplin's later films, such as *The Great Dictator* where he plays two roles, Hitler and a Jewish barber, based on identical looks, but, though brilliant as the film is, the paradox of these two people being physically identical and in *real life* one and the same person, pushed paradox to an extreme that was difficulty to tolerate or accept; and any attempts at comic relief in that film left many uneasy.

Of course, this in fact may have been illustrative of Chaplin's two sides. One conscious, the other unconscious?

Cinema audiences, of course, are not analysts. In therapy, this would be an important issue to deal with.

Paradox and the balance of fantasy with reality

We live in two worlds, that of fantasy and that of reality. It seems to me that both worlds are indispensable to the enjoyment and appreciation of human experience and development. These worlds are also paradoxical, in that under some circumstances one may obviate the other, yet they are both "always there." The level of comfort we have with both, and their intertwining, is a strong determinant of not only our personality structure, but of our attitude toward life.

Unconscious affects, internalizations, defensive structures, and traumas, of course, play an enormous role in influencing the relative interpenetration or dissociation of fantasy and reality in our personal development. For one thing, it leads to the acceptance or the disavowal of what Winnicott (1971) termed "potential space." It is my position that disavowal of potential space can lead to over-idealization of objective reality and its derivative "the factual" which, in the extreme, can lead to a rather dry non-playful human. Under such a condition, the aesthetic quality of any relationship is lost. Disavowal of potential space can also, in an opposite extreme, motivate a tendency to become so deeply immersed in valuing the illusional such that a person is just "not in touch."[2]

Given the above, I will suggest that the direction and process of human development is not away from the illusional, but rather towards putting the illusional in an ever more integrated perspective, a perspective which leads to an ever-increasing ability to accept paradox as a fundamental

---

2 As in such current beliefs in crystals, astrology, psychics, over-idealization of a partner, etc.

quality of human experience. The concept of paradox goes back a long way in psychology, as well as in other fields such as physics. For example, to physicists such as Bohr and Heisenberg, the notion of paradox implicit in the uncertainty principle and the concept of indeterminacy (the very act of observing influences what we observed, thus we can never obtain a "true" observation) was used in arguments with Einstein over the possibility of a strictly measurable and analyzable universe , (Clark 1971, pp. 341–343). In psychology, this notion was early on understood by William James (1890) who "observed an important paradox: when the continuity that characterizes the stream of consciousness is interrupted by observation, there is a disjunction between the experiencing and observing mind" (Modell 1990, p. 55). Social psychologists influenced by the work of Kurt Lewin (1943), such as Barker (1968) and Schoggen (1989), also were interested in understanding the "Stream of Behavior" and how to divide this "stream" into meaningful segments. Their attempts to develop an "ecological psychology" to resolve the incommensurate laws governing "extra-individual, wave patterns of behavior, tied to particular parts of the physical-temporal-geographic environment (Schoggen 1989, p. vii) with those governing individual, internal, idiosyncratic qualities were only partially successful. To draw an analogy from physics and the concept of complementarity, we may say that just as light is both paradoxically a wave and a particle, depending upon the context by which it is studied or understood (Clark 1971, p. 342), so too are human beings metaphorically waves or particles, depending upon our context of understanding. *At one level we are quite alike, but at another level we are all different; similarly, in the clinical setting, at one level each session is unique; at another, it is embedded in the context of previous sessions. Still again, at one level we are continuous through time, at another we are always "in the moment."* It thus seems that the way to understand a person greatly depends upon the level of inquiry and interest, and the particular context in which such inquiry is embedded. In my own work, I have drawn from the cinematic concept of montage, as to how we arrange "the therapeutic scene" in terms of what is emphasized and indeed what is created and experienced (Brok, 2014). In a way, analogous to a movie director's attempts at montage and continuity, researchers from various scientific disciplines have been interested in how we organize human behavior and its communication into meaningful segments; at question is not only who does the organizing, but also how we understand the influence of the organizing process itself! The analogy to the therapeutic process and the influence of such models for technique as the relational (Mitchell, 1991), the intersubjective (Stolorow and Atwood, 1992), as well as the work on the psychodynamic field by the Barangers (2008) is I trust obvious. These issues have incrementally become significant in the analytic literature.

In the analytical literature on paradox, we have of course the work initiated by Winnicott (1971, p. xii) and followed up such authors as Modell (1990, 2003) and Mitchell (1991) and Pizer (1992), as psychoanalysis has integrated subjective experience and two-person psychology in its theory of clinical technique. I am hoping that my work adds to the significance of all of the above within a broader developmental-ecological framework. Implicit in this is the notion of *context,* which, as I define it, includes topology (the psychological field at any given moment as experienced by the self), intrapsychic phenomena (internalized object relations, id, ego, ego-ideal, superego, and ego ideal interactions and self–object needs), one's personal archaeology (particular genetic history and encoded affects), and the historical-cultural milieu in which all this is embedded.[3]

---

3 Interestingly, a recent report on quantum computers "which move beyond understanding that bits of information hold a binary value of either 1 or 0, by "accepting the notion that a single object (bit) can behave like two separate objects at the same time when it is either extremely small or extremely cold." (*New York Times*, Oct 24, 2019). Context seems to be extremely important in understanding all sorts of things, including human behavior. This could be quite daunting for those who need a sense of consistency with no paradoxical deviations. How much paradox can be accepted is an important issue in human relations. *Where it is denied and devalued can be just as problematic as witnessing extremely inconsistent behavior; something I will suggest Chaplin the shadow via his screen* **persona** *was wrestling with in his later work.* Chaplin the person was relatively consistent and coherent in his final and long-term relationship with Oona O'Neill. While in his film work, he played two distinct personalities in *The Great Dictator*, as well as in *Monsieur Verdoux*. While in *Limelight* and *A King in New York*, as well as the aforementioned earlier films, he intertwined serious political issues with attempts to maintain play/ humor and slapstick comedy. In addition to the political messages that some of the audience was not ready for, his insertion of play/humor into the seriousness of his work also seems to have alienated a portion of his audience. He also showed complex paradoxical feelings towards women, being tender with some and killing others as the protagonist in *Monsieur Verdoux*, or assaulting them in *A King in New York*, as he struggled with his own aging on screen, but not quite the same way in real life as we shall see in later chapters.

CHAPTER 2

Locating Play

Discovering where play is located in the geography of our life experience is highly dependent on the searcher's perspective. For some, play is located in our childhood experience and is slowly but surely outgrown. Others note that play remains with us as a way of being through adulthood, but in greatly transformed form, such as creativity. Play and its cousin humor have been located as a function, such as the ego's attempt to master trauma[4], while others locate play as existing in the spontaneous enjoyment of intrinsically motivated activities. In sum, play has a history of many definitions and ascribed functions.

Within psychodynamic thinking, Winnicott's ideas were the first extended attempt to discuss the relevance of play as both an attitude and process. Winnicott was explicit in stating that play was a fundamental

---

4 One example is in the award-winning film *Life is Beautiful* (1998) which highlighted play in the service of disavowal and triumph over traumatic reality.

quality of human experience and that it provides for many unique and productive human processes.

It is play that is universal and belongs to health, playing facilitates growth and therefore health; playing leads into group relationship; playing can be a form of communication in psychotherapy; and psychoanalysis has been developed as a very specialized form of playing in the service of communication to one's self and others, (Winnicott, 1971)

Although Winnicott's perspective is quite profound, clinical experience tells us that play can also be a source of resistance to the insight so necessary for the therapeutic process to unfold in all its depth. In the clinical situation, it would seem that play as a state and as a process could be in opposition to the rational function in the analytic search for meaning, as well as an amplifier *and creator* of meaning when it emerges and is appropriately experienced within a given session. (As we shall see in the case of Assistant Professor L., later in this work.)

Anderegg (1989), in an attempt to clarify Winnicott's notions of play, suggests that in a "general sense, for Winnicott, playing involves the intrapsychic manipulation of reality; playing becomes a synonym for representation" (1989, p. 559). For Winnicott, it seems, only after representation is achieved can playing become interactive. Ego-relatedness must precede object-relatedness. The experience of two people playing together can only come after a period where one person (prototypically the infant) plays alone with proto-symbols, in the presence of the other, prototypically the mother. I would amend Winnicott's position of "presence' to *the experienced sense of the other (usually the mother) as an involved, non-impinging witness.*

Play, for Winnicott, occurs in "potential space." Potential space may be conceived as an area of paradoxical experience in which the infant operates on an intrapsychic level between " me – extensions and not – me." Potential space may also be conceived of as an area of illusion, a reality different from that of ordinary life (Modell 1991).

Literality Destroys Play

The ability for playful interaction is dependent upon one's capacity to signal non – literality of communication and to recognize non – literality by the other. Simply put, the attribution of something as literal when it is intended to be experienced as non-literal will destroy the play experience. Focusing on the literality inherent in something intended to be non-literal obfuscates the playful moment. Bateson (1955) called this characteristic "alluding to the playframe."

For example, a good way to eliminate the joy of watching a magician perform his tricks is to take his performance as a literal as opposed to a non-literal communication to his audience. When one says, "That is impossible, I'm not going to pretend it's magic," we move from wonder and joy, to science and reality.

Literality in the Clinical Situation

In the clinical situation there are those individuals who have an internal need to tenaciously cling to literality; while others have too strongly cathected illusion. It seems that for the former, early adoptive needs have required them to over rely on the rational and intellectual while desperately avoiding the reality of the irrational and illusional, lest they be lost within it. The symbolic, metaphorical, and spontaneous registers of experience were not available. One such patient I have described elsewhere (Brok 1982) could not lie on the couch until her third year of analytic treatment. She took the experience vis à vis my sitting behind her as a literal representation of being with an uninvolved and highly narcissistic mother. This patient could not allow herself or, better put, did not have the tools to use the analytic process as a play space, as she seemed to have no significant database for the experience of being in a "play state" with either parent. For her, early impingements pushed the capacity for a sustained sense of potential space out of the realm of possibility. Another patient, an incest victim, made significant progress at the point that she could suspend the internal literal meaning of lying down on the couch of a "male," even though she recognized he was a therapist, for the paradoxical and, to her, the ambiguous experience of feeling "as if" she were in a potentially dangerous incestuous situation. We both knew she was not, but she could now "play" with the feeling. It was at this point that my patient could experience the transference as a "transference" and not a literal recapitulation of past reality. As we can note, "play" is not always joyful. It is simply an important state to have in one's repertoire of being.

Some patients use the literality of the professional setting to avoid the invitation by the analyst to use one's experience and fantasy in a therapeutically meaningful way. When the latter is not possible, the analytic space becomes a playframe that is constantly alluded to in the service of defense, resistance, or simply not developmentally available. Such patients need and take a lot of time to develop a sense of trust and recoup a sense of being in potential space rather than avoiding it. The process is not unilateral, as it takes considerable awareness by the therapist to develop a climate where constraints in the relational field are lowered sufficiently for comfort with mutuality to be experienced. One such patient, a man who had been abandoned as a young adolescent and literally lived in the woods for a short time until taken in by a surrogate mother, has been seeing me for seven years off and on. Now in adulthood, he was self-made, highly competent, supremely rational, and coming off as not needing anyone, while paradoxically maintaining a relationship with me for many years. As our therapeutic relationship evolved, he slowly and incrementally began taking notes about his thoughts about himself that he shared with me. "Am I afraid not to be 'alone?'" "Do I not trust my judgement?" "Am I avoiding intimacy?" In effect. he was playing with ideas rather than always being focused on facts.

Interpenetration

As I have noted previously, some patients seem to have never learned to play. Early adaptive needs seem to push them towards two defensive styles. One being an overreliance on illusion, the other being a rigidified need to hold on to a joyless significance of reality at all cost. For the former, the affect of joy and the enchantment of play become transformed into an illusory denial of reality; while for the latter, play, illusion, and affect related to these experiences become subservient to a psychic fealty to what is rational and literal. The healthy individual, I would suggest, has developed a capacity to integrate, separate, and interpenetrate play and reality, without fear of losing his bearing either cognitively or affectively.[5] Irving (2019) has recently discussed this capacity as "elational agility," while I have discussed this capacity as developing/allowing a broader repertoire of potential ways of being to evolve… much like an actor sufficiently comfortable with himself can do improvisation without overidentifying with the various roles/ways of being in his performance. One example of the overidentifying I am discussing can be seen in the excellent performance by Natalie Portman as a ballerina and principal protagonist in the film *Black Swan* where, in the film, she actually dies at the end, a sad metaphor for her taking things too concretely as opposed to being able to see her ballet role as one of many play states in her repertoire of being.

Bach also has recently alluded to the capacity for experiencing an interpenetration of objective and subjective self-states in his work on "States of Self Surrender." He notes that "in order to maintain a balanced sense of our existence, self-experience must alternate and interpenetrate with self-observation in a continuous process of oscillation free of traumatic constraints" (Bach 2019). Balint has also made interesting reference to the concept of interpenetration. To quote, "The analyst must be indestructible, and he must allow his patient to live with him in a sort of harmonious interpenetrating mix up." (Balint 1968, p. 136.) Modell (1990), in reaction to this quote, states, "This harmonious interpenetrating mix up is reminiscent of what Kohut (1977) would later describe as the self-object transference."

---

5   By interpenetrate, I mean something kindred to the acceptance of paradox as opposed to the notion of integration, which has to do with the ego's need to synthesize.

I would disagree, and term it more as a healthy/ intersubjective transference/ reality experience.

Some Further thoughts on Play

I have been thinking that play, among its other definitions, may be conceived of as a state of illusion-acceptance in which a person may momentarily enter into as the context in which play occurs, without losing the capacity to experience a sense of reality. Reality in play is not so much suspended as "furloughed." By this I mean reality becomes a non-impinging background stimulus that is not attended to (different than defended against) in deference to the singular contextual significance of the momentary state. Like the prototypical mother who is always there, reality provides the necessary holding environment (contextual system) which encourages the free autonomous state of play to flourish within its boundaries. In this sense, play is not an illusion, conceived as a state independent of reality, but rather a special class of illusion, illusional experience-which-can-be-enjoyed within reality. An ego state, (an originally pristine ego state) if you will, that is in confluence with the id and not overwhelmed or defended against because it is not interfered with, but rather is co-experienced in its context by an empathic witness (an empathic witness that is internalized or external and serves as a supportive sustaining structure). As a result, there is no requirement for the *active* presence of either a primitive super-ego or an oedipal super-ego. In adults, a play state then is an autonomous ego state free to expand in the direction of the id under the benign super-ego's passive auspices. Another way of putting it is to say that the ego is autonomous within its intra-psychic system without being independent of it, such that the illusional (as in make-believe) and the non-rational is acceptable and entered into but always embedded (located) within the reality social system. This is also a basis for creative experience and action, and I daresay an actor with a wide repertoire of being on stage does this without losing himself.

For adults, play is a product of the ego's choice to access a previously enjoyable sense of experience. But now, like the proverbial farm boy who returns to his home after living in the city, things are not exactly the same. For, as adults, we experience regression with the experience of progression already within us. We now choose to enter states that were previously a choiceless "given," and as a result we do lose some the joyous wonder we had as children and infants. Luckily for many of us, we can sufficiently recapture its essence.

A Thesis About Play and the Media

In the media, depiction and communication of playful topics and joyful experience trade on our acceptance as an audience to the artist's invitation for us to "be in" potential space" with his work. However, the closer the topic presented is to our immediate fear or active conflicts, the more difficult it is for us to identify with the playful/aesthetic element and enjoy or appreciate the experience. We cannot be "in the moment" because we are so aware of the facts (the facts of our past and subjective experiences/perceptions, as well as the objective facts of any given situation.)

As we shall see in the clinical chapters, I will propose the existence of an "aesthetic therapeutic contract" between analyst and patient which is an analogue of the film artist's communication with his audience. Of course, the clinical relationship, unlike that of a film, involves here-and-now interaction with mutual intersubjective and objective receptivity between two participants, albeit with differing roles. However, the analyst as audience to the patient's play communication, and the response he makes, can be crucial for the quality and progress of the clinical relationship. The reverse applies under appropriate circumstances. (This holds for humor/ jokes too.)

In light of the above, my thesis, which I will unpack in the next chapter, is that Chaplin's attempts at political/social realism in his later films reduced the efficacy of his play element, which in turn reduced the audience's capacity to appreciate and enjoy the full significance of his art – at particular points in social time. Playful audience participation and stressful/traumatizing topics cannot coexist easily or comfortably. Thus, we shall see that in Chaplin's film relation to his audience, potential space was overwhelmed by the literal quality of reality.

CHAPTER 3

Chaplin: The Playful Element in His Films

The filmmaking career of Charles Chaplin was one of the longest and most striking of the twentieth century. Spanning a period of fifty-three years, from 1914–1967, Chaplin appeared in at least 81 films – the vast majority of which he wrote, produced, and directed as well as played the principal role. A remarkable feat by a man who retained remarkable control over his screen productions, his "little tramp" was and may still be the most recognizable and known screen image throughout the world.

If one follows Chaplin's development as a film artist, it seems that his ability to communicate poignant and often serious messages to his audience through films peppered with playful and comical activity diminished greatly in the United States as a function of the cultural-political climate of the time. It appears that a disjunction occurred between Chaplin and segments of his audience at certain moments in history. The playful, non-literal part of his aesthetic contract with his audience greatly diminished as he increasingly attempted to communicate more literal and "experience near" political/social messages through his film productions. Play in the foreground can only occur when reality is in the background. I am suggesting that Chaplin's increasing focus on "experience near" social reality in his later films, created foreground out of background and diminished the role of play/humor as an effective form of communication. His films began to contain social themes that beckoned the rational to the forefront. They became politically significant stories to follow rather than discrete comical episodes and events embedded in human pathos and folly. Specifically, it seems that Chaplin's social messages aroused anxiety due to the "experience near" fears and righteously held beliefs in his audience at that time. This was, of course, not for all the individuals in his audience, but indeed, for many, it created quite a controversy. What were these fears and beliefs?

1. Chaplin must be a Communist. (*Modern Times*, 1936) (*A King in New York*, 1957)
2. He wants to get us into a war. (*The Great Dictator*, 1940)
3. He challenges our basic "goodness" (*Monsieur Verdoux*, 1947)
4. He can destabilize = traumatize = create conflict with our hoped-for allies in South America. For example, Argentina banned *The Great Dictator* when it came out, and President Roosevelt had actually asked him not to produce the film as he worried about its political impact on parts of Latin America that were supposedly neutral but clearly Pro-Axis (*Buenos Aire*s Herald 1940, pp. 1 and 4).

This was a time of considerable isolationist sentiment in the United States, as well as the U.S. government's and media's attempts to keep South America positively connected to the country. For example, the "Good Neighbor Policy" and popular Hollywood films stressing positive though simple ideas about South America, such as *Flying down to Rio* (1933), *Down Argentine Way* (1940) with Betty Grable and Don Ameche and Carmen Miranda, were some of the exemplars of this. Also, there were such historical endeavors as the Pan American Union.

Thus, *Modern Times* (1936), a critique of big industry, was not enjoyed by many who just wanted Chaplin to play "The Little Tramp" he was so well known for. This departure to progressive social messages interpenetrated with comedy was felt to be too paradoxical for many to tolerate. *The Great Dictator* (1940) was panned by many critics who were isolationist, while others felt it too serious a topic to burlesque and too naïve in its illusory ending. Bosley Crowther, respected film reviewer for the *New York Times* in those years recalls that:

> The Great Dictator *was in production when the war began (in Europe). Chaplin was in a quandary. Should he abandon it or go on? Had the monstrousness of Hitler become too sinister for jokes or would ridicule still be effective in exposing the monstrosity of the man? Chaplin decided to continue. But when the film was released in October 1940, the war had taken an ominous turn and critics were of the opinion that the time for laughing at Hitler was past. Although Chaplin superbly mimics the mincing mannerisms and shouting oratory of the demagogue, the film*

struck too many people as insensitive and distasteful at the time. Chaplin was criticized for it, which evidently hurt him very much. (Crowther 1964, p.18)

Picture 1. The Great Dictator, Copyright Roy Export S.A.S.

Picture 2. The Great Dictator, Copyright Roy Export, S.A.S.

Picture 3. The Great Dictator, Copyright Roy Export, S.A.S.

Picture 4. The Great Dictator, Copyright Roy Export, S.A.S.

In *The Great Dictator*, Chaplin brilliantly plays *two paradoxical roles* – that of Hitler and that of a Jewish barber. The Jewish barber, a former World War I hero, suffers from amnesia and has been in a sanitarium. It is now the late 1930s and the barber is released from the sanitarium. As he returns to open his dusty unused barber shop, he has no sense that persecution of Jews is in full force. There are many brilliant scenes in this film. Here I excerpt one to illustrate the notion that play and *serious immediate* social reality experience do not interact well. The scene is a choreographed sequence towards which audiences to this very day encounter with mixed feelings.

Charlie as the Jewish barber gets into a tussle defending his right to rub out the word "JEW" scrawled on his storefront. A storm trooper seizes him. Charlie, believing he has rights, appeals to another "policeman" to arrest the storm trooper. Instead of helping, the second trooper tries to grab Charlie. There is a tussle. Paulette Goddard (playing a young Jewish woman) appears at the window overlooking the sidewalk and sees the tussle going on below.

Recognizing Charlie, she grabs a large pan, reaches out the window, and bangs the storm trooper on the head. The tussle below goes on and she errantly smashes Charlie on the head as well. What then ensues is a ballet-like erratic sequence in which Charlie dazedly wanders up and down the street, running and stumbling off and on the sidewalk in a stupor. Taken out of context, it is quite funny; Charlie is a brilliant dancer and looks a little bit like a drunken Gene Kelly in the subsequently famous *Singing in the Rain* (1952) film sequence. (I wonder if Kelly got the idea from Charlie's film?) What is not so funny to many people, especially Jewish audiences, even to this day, is that Charlie's tripping dance takes him past a multitude of store windows and walls with the label "JEW" scrawled in paint on them.

Charlie winds up in the arms of the storm trooper and, again, eventually staggers to the ground.[6]

Chaplin's next film, *Monsieur Verdoux* (1947), was misunderstood and objected to by many when it was released. I would suggest this was due to the increased literality of Chaplin's communication, both on his part and in the perception of his art by his audience. In this film, which is set in France, Chaplin portrays an unemployed bank clerk, a victim of the depression who becomes a serial killer. He is a Bluebeard who seduces, marries, and then murders women to collect their money, ostensibly to provide for his crippled wife and child. When finally caught, he argues in his defense that he is no different, if not better, than "nations who kill millions with nuclear weapons." Believing that, after all, he was "just doing business," only on a smaller level than a warring nation. He goes on to refer to nuclear weapons, dryly saying that when it comes to killing, "*numbers sanctify*." His claim that it is unjust for him to be condemned as a criminal, while a soldier who murders in the name of his country is proclaimed a hero. Ultimately, he is judged guilty, and the film ends with his being taken to the guillotine. Although he inserts a number of playful/humorous slapstick sections in the film, the total "feel" of the visual and spoken narrative is sinister, cynical, and ironically bitter. Why he inserts these slapstick pieces is hard to fathom, other than that they are crude attempts to keep two paradoxical sides of his persona available for all to see. This paradox would be understood by an analyst hopefully but not by his audience, who found again the sinister and political message of this film

---

6 What is brilliant about this scene is, I think, the communication of Charlie as the protagonist describing in motion how the Jewish world in Germany was turned upside down and disorientingly crazy –making. In that context, it is brilliant, but not funny.

too hard to view as a comedy with a message. Below are stills from *Monsieur Verdoux*. The first one is with one of his wives, acted by Martha Ray, who he gets into a supposedly comic tussle in a rowboat as he tries to murder her by strangling, only to ineptly stumble around and eventually fall off the boat.

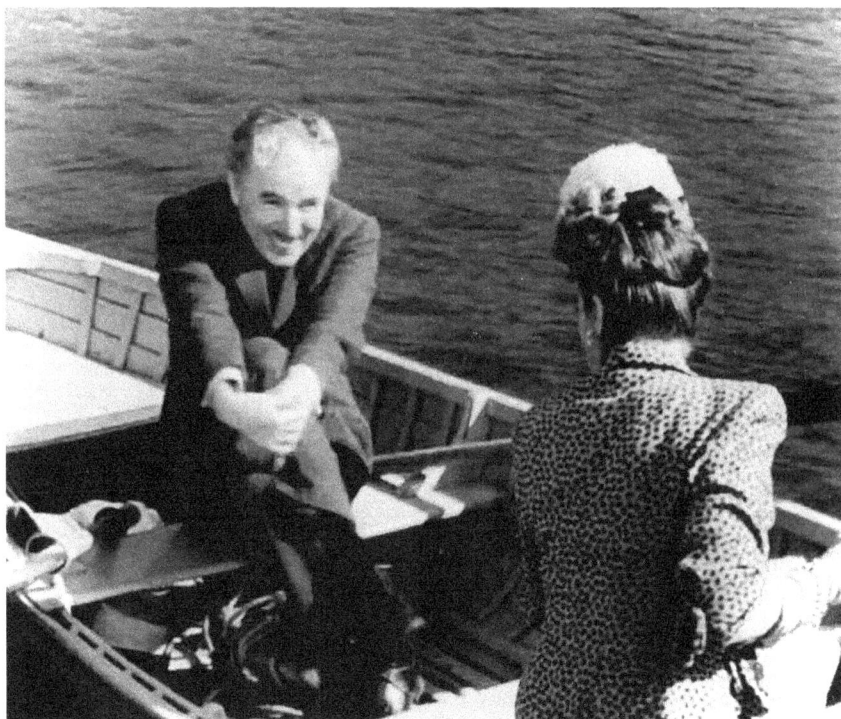

Picture 5.Monsieur Verdeoux, Copyright Roy Export, S.A.S.

Picture 6. Monsieur Verdoux copyright: Roy Export, S.A.S.

Picture 7. Monsieur Verdoux Copyright, Roy Export. S.A.S.

In the above still, he has befriended a 'lost woman" who he brings to his quarters to test out a poison. However, he takes pity on her because she is so pretty and has a criminal background he seems to identify with. With a series of comic maneuvers, he does not give her the wine containing the deadly substance, by switching glasses. In another scene, he shakes with fear that he has accidently drunken the wine with poison intended for one of his many rich wives. Here played by Martha Ray.

Picture 8. Monsieur Verdoux, copyright Roy Export, S.A.S.

As background, let me briefly allude to Chaplin's real-life situation at the time he made *Monsieur Verdoux* in 1947. David Robinson, one of his biographers, notes:

Life had altered for Chaplin. The absurd, humiliating law suits involved in the paternity charge of Joan Barry, as well as the growing atmosphere of political paranoia surrounding the sittings of the House Un-American Activities Committee, had suddenly toppled him from the heights of popularity that he had enjoyed for thirty-eight years. From being the best loved man in America, he had become the most excoriated. A congressman waged a campaign to have his "loathsome pictures" banned from exhibition: and there were all too many to support it. (Robinson 1983)[7] See Newspaper headline below from the Chicago Daily Tribune.

Picture 9. Copyright Chicago Tribune

---

7 Weismann, S.M. (2008). In his excellent book, *Chaplin: A Life*, which emphasizes Chaplin's early career, though giving short shrift to his later more serious films, has noted that the making of *Monsieur Verdoux* might have to do with his anger at women, in particular towards Joan Barry, and that he uses film to kill where he cannot in reality. Though plausible, I think that Weismann minimizes the combination of complex factors that lead Charlie to make the film, including an unconscious critique of his psychotic mother, inadequate family, and impingement of the McCarthy Un-American hearings, etc. The United States had in some sense become a Fatherland that failed him, even though he was ambivalently attached, having never become a U.S. Citizen.

Picture 10. Monsieur Verdoux, copyright Roy Export, S.A.S.
Monsieur Verdoux on trial for his murders of many women,
who he married to get their funds.

Chaplin's next film, *Limelight* (1952), acclaimed by many and misunderstood by some, was to my mind a strongly autobiographical film about the real Chaplin's bitterness. It remains a masterpiece on the poignant issues of aging and loss of popularity, as well as a depiction of him being a hero who saves a young actress from despair and suicide. In so doing, he is keeping the spark of hope and life he seems to have lost alive in her. Eventually, he will lose/ let her go, to a young handsome actor. Unlike his little tramp films, or even *Modern Times*, Chaplin does not end up with the girl. This cinema ending is quite different than Chaplin's actual life, where he is married to Oona,

36 years younger than him, already with a number of children. In the film we see a Chaplin, no longer a popular comedian, waxing philosophically about life, love, fame and even a bit about Freud. His bitterness is reflected in such quotes in the film, as he speaks in a thoughtful aside to the young actress who he has saved from despair and suicide, clearly about his own lost audiences, "*the public is a monster without a head…that never knows which way it is going to turn, and can be prodded in any direction." (Limelight, 1952)* This is one of many philosophical intellectual riffs about life that are in apposition to the bits of comedy that are later part of the film. At one point, Claire Bloom, who plays the young actress he saved from suicide and despair, says to him in a poignant part of the script. "*To hear you talk, no one would ever think you were a* comedian." It would seem that Chaplin indeed was using the cinema screen to project and reflect and deal with anguished personal issues, such as rejection by some of his cinematic audience, aging and dying. In the end of the film he does die: while in reality he is very much alive in his real life in Switzerland. Below, see a picture of Chaplin as Calvero, lecturing about life to Clare Bloom, the young actress he saves from suicide and eventually cedes to a younger man, as he (Calvero) dies during a theatrical comedy comeback.

Picture 11. Limelight, Copyright Roy Export, S.A.S.

As Walter Kerr, a well-known critic of that time, has noted: "Chaplin was a *"profound clown – the greatest, most beloved we have – is seeking a second reputation as a sage. It is not likely to equal his first." (Focus on Chaplin, Edited by D. W. McCaffrey 1971, p. 148).* Nevertheless, there are attempts at comedy in this film, which remain sad and incongruous, rather than the sparkling and spicy slapstick of his previous films. This is quite in opposition to his real-life experience with being an oedipal winner and "getting the younger girl" in his marriage to Oona! In *Limelight* we also see displaced onto the screen, his sense of recapturing and trying to cure his young psychotic mother, and what looks like an overidentification with his father, (a drunken, Music hall actor and singer of some renown, who was separated from Charlie's mother and died at an early age) who Chaplin will in real life outlive by some 50 years. From the point of view of the thesis of this book, comic humor and play is not always appreciated by an audience that feels it is out of context.

Picture 12. Limelight, Copyright, Roy Export, S.A.S.

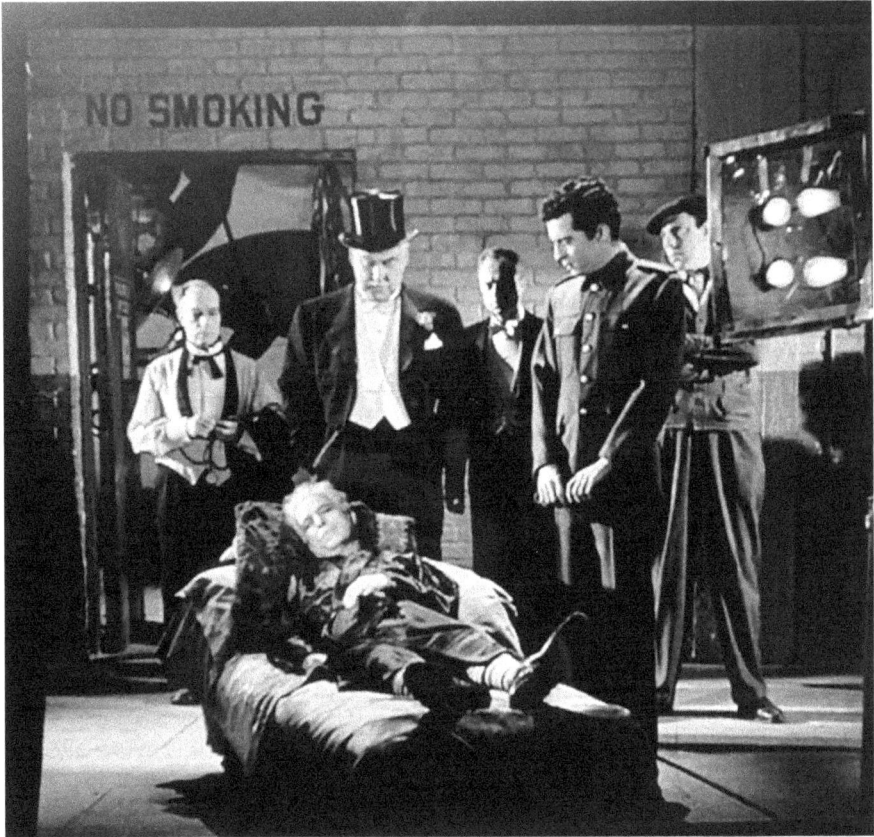

Picture 13. Limelight, Copyright, Roy Export, S.A.S.

Finally, *A King in New York* (1957) was an angry invective at the House Un-American Activities Committee. Though laced with jokes and slapstick humor, these films were more and more conveying serious social themes. The slapstick, now attempted by an old and much less nimble Chaplin, is sad to watch, really not fitting in with the theme of the film. He plays an exiled king from a European country, now broke, and in the United States and wanting to use atomic energy for peaceful purposes. The film narrative turns on many critiques of American advertising techniques and culture. He himself, to obtain money, makes a botched commercial for "Royal Crown Whiskey," where he chokes on the product, which ironically becomes a comic hit. There are many unsettling supposedly comic bits in the film, one such in the picture below, where, in character as King Shadov, sitting between an attractive woman he is interested in and an elderly talkative woman sitting beside him at a formal dinner, he abuses the latter, grabbing her crudely and pouring a huge amount of wine on her face as well as shoving utensils into her mouth. (see picture #16, below) This slapstick technique reflects an inner sadism and a split between an idealized hunger for younger attractive women an imago of his mother, who he never gave up on being with, and the imago's realization via his real relationship with Oona. In this film, the attractive woman he meets is quite calculating, played by Dawn Addams, as a TV director who fends off the sexual advances of King Shadov. but becomes his friend and involves him in various commercial activities. Towards the end of the film, after being investigated by the House Un-American Actvities , Chaplin, in his role as King, decides to leave the United States. As they part, she says about the HUAC investigations, "*It's only a passing phase,*" and his response is, "*I've had enough, I will sit it out in Europe.*" Which reflects the real Chaplin's feelings and actions who at the time of the film was already living in Switzerland.

Pictures 14, 15 A King in New York Copyright Roy Export.S.A.S.

Picture 16. A King in New York, Copyright Roy Export, S.A.S.

Picture 17. A King in New York, Copyright, Roy Export, S.A.S.

There are many attempts at comic/playful moments inserted in this serious film that is severely critical of American culture and politics. Above we see one such as he is served a subpoena to the HUAC hearings and somehow gets his finger stuck in a fire hose and cannot get it out, winding up going to the hearings with the fire hose attached to him.

The audience for these films at that time in cultural-political history could not easily play with Chaplin's ideas and thereby feel safe enough to absorb his message (with the exception of *Limelight* – which features a less controversial, more nostalgic, though tragic theme). Further, the attempted comic/ play element in these films could not balance the experience- near impact of the events depicted. In Chaplin's film relation with his audience, potential space was overwhelmed by the literal quality of real space.

A Thought About Chaplin's Motives

The movie theatre for Chaplin's audience became not a holding environment, but rather a place to receive verbal interpretive information about the audience's own culture and society. His films were received as an interpretive communication that were seen as Chaplin's realistic bitterness and cynicism, as well as a comment about his perception of the reality of his audience's culture and society. In short, Chaplin's later films became politically significant stories to follow, rather than discrete comical episodes and events embedded in themes of pathos and folly.

But why did he make these later films? On one level, they were clearly ideological messages. From 1936 on, his films became progressively more serious and verbal (fully verbal starting in 1940).[8] On another level, as seen above, they were responses to his audience's reactions to his life dilemmas. On a third level, they were attempts to enable the progress of a stifled and arrested self-development. The shadow of Chaplin the man that we see, especially in his later works, is derived from the substance of his self-projected and worked over feelings in a public manner through the dreamlike medium of film. Never in psychoanalysis, Chaplin used his films as containers to hold and/or rework his personal issues.[9] His ability to do this, I think, was crucial to his relatively successful emotional development throughout the stream of his life.

What I shall argue in subsequent sections is that Chaplin was trying to "work out" in public space, via his films, issues and conflicts which were disturbing his private self. Instead of disengaging, he was attempting to remain engaged. His was a creative solution to his issues through the medium of film. Many artists use their art in this manner, and it is credible that Chaplin used his art in this way early on. See for example a brief discussion by Modell (1993 pp. 90–91) of *City Lights,* and the same can be said for *The Kid* (Weissmann, 2008, pp 3–4, 53, 263). The point I am making is that in his silent films Chaplin's attempt to deal with private issues were greatly disguised, i.e. one had to literally be an analyst with

---

8 In *Modern Times* (1936), every protagonist talks except for Chaplin. His voice is however heard once in a babble, as a singing waiter. Almost like a child's babble that indicates he is getting ready to speak.

9 For example, in *Limelight,* he plays the role of an old and unappreciated actor who indeed saves a young desperate actress from dying, but eventually gives her up to a younger protagonist. In effect accepting oedipal loss in fantasy, while in fact he had won a major oedipal victory in real life by marrying Oona O'Neill, some 36 years younger than him and daughter of Eugene O'Neill who despised Charlie. Oona, as I suggest, was also a healthy version of his psychotic mother.

sufficient information to understand the depth of Chaplin's seriousness in his comedy. As a result, the majority of his audience could indirectly identify with the pathos in his early films without feeling threatened. Only later, when Chaplin went on to more overt social and political themes did he begin to lose significant segments of his audience. He began to let his private persona "hang out" in the public domain.

Talking: A Developmental Step

Of importance to understanding Chaplin is the role of "talkies," as sound film came to be called in the late 1920s and early thirties. Spoken language is a significant form of communication and is especially important for communication of rational experience, depiction of reality, interpersonal comprehension of intended meaning, or intellectual ideas, etc. In short, verbal mastery is a significant ego function. Both early babble and nonverbal states and communications are "languages of direct emotion." One can directly experience the feeling state depicted by a dancer, pantomime artist, or babbling child. The experience is decidedly less rational than clear verbal communication. In comparison to nonverbal communication, verbal communication tends be more cognitive than affective. There is also a quality of universality that can be attributed to nonverbal communication. Chaplin's own description of his reticence to use speech in his films is as follows:

Only the curious would want to hear me speak, anyway, but millions want no change. Of that I am convinced, pantomime is the oldest art... the good book says that in the beginning was the word, but people understood each other by signs before they did sounds. And I expect understood each other better. Someone wrote words were given us to conceal our thoughts. Words can defeat the imagination, they destroy the illusion. People can be moved more intensely by gesture than by voice. I am not speaking of singing, singing is divine. I am speaking of the actor who can speak. In the appeal to emotions, the silent clown with his pantomime can beat the throaty tragedian every time. (Chaplin, quoted in Haining 1983, pp. 106-107).

It is in keeping with my thesis that when Chaplin did finally relinquish his reticence about talking, the thematic organization of his films began to change. Chaplin moved from themes of play, slapstick comedy, and pathos to themes of bitter, angry, cynical humor, reflecting his thoughts about both current society and his need for self-examination and his own adult development. Idealistic themes juxtaposed with pessimistic ones emerge as Chaplin wavers between naïve appeals for peace and sensitivity, in the ending of *The Great Dictator*, and sardonic social/political commentary in the ending of *Monsieur Verdoux*.

Dualities persist even within his films – such as the *The Great Dictator*. As noted earlier, Chaplin plays a dual role, both Hitler and a Jew. Identical-looking film characters with distinct personalities. One taken with fantasy and grandiosity (Hitler), the other proud and naively idealistic (the Jew). In the film, they are both mistakenly identified for each other. The film ends with the Jew in Hitler's place giving an evocative and naïve illusory plea for peace. Are these Chaplin's two sides?

As I noted above, in his very next film, *Monsieur Verdoux*, Chaplin plays a serial killer who murders the women he marries in order to inherit their fortunes – all for the "noble purpose" of supporting his invalid wife and children. The film ends with his going to the guillotine after a sharp biting condemnation of society. An ending of very sharp contrast to the idealistic final scene of *The Great Dictator!* I suggest, that taken in tandem, these two films exemplify Chaplin's inner conflicts and dualities. Embedded like the Russian children's toy of a doll within a doll, Chaplin's inner conflicts can be seen embedded both within and between his later films. What were these conflicts?

It seems to me that the latent meaning behind Chaplin's delayed transition to speech in his films has to do with a slow but incremental disengagement from a powerful need to maintain an omnipotent fusion between his ego and ego – ideal. Following the work of Chasseguet-Smirgel (1985), I suggest that Chaplin had great difficulty giving up the wish to re-fuse with an illusionary mother, and was only partially to succeed through his final marriage to a displaced though, rational version of his psychotic fantasy-fulfilling early mother. His marriage to Oona O'Neill would serve him well as a near perfect self – object. Just as his holding on, and/or trying to save "injured" young women in his later films would also reflect this.

In sum, in using speech, he was evolving developmentally, moving from his early fantasy mother to his later disappointing mother and towards the more rational world of his somewhat functional but abandoning father. *All his later films make us think, rather than play/ or laugh, yet ask us to still accept laughing,* and for those of us who cannot tolerate this, the paradox is difficult. What we are forced to think about and also laugh about becomes an aversive experience. Of interest to my thesis is that Chaplin himself recognized that he may be going overboard. For example, in *A King in New York*, there is a young boy whose parents are being investigated by the House Un-American Activities Committee. The young protagonist, who is over-intellectualized and politically idealistic, is played by one of his actual sons, Michael. His parents are being investigated by HUAC. In a crucial scene, Chaplin, the King in New York, advises him, "*You think too much, you should play more.*" As if talking to himself, and I believe, reminiscing about the "good old days" of his non-political cinema themes as the little tramp.

Picture 18. A King in New York, Copyright Roy Export, S.A.S.

Picture 19. A King in New York, Copyright Roy Export, S.A.S.

Pictures 20, 21. A King in New York, Copyright Roy Export, S.A.S.

Picture 22. A King in New York, Copyright Roy Export, S.A.S.

Chaplin: Personal Self-Development

Starting with the unintelligible babble of the singing waiter in *Modern Times*, through the sharp and idealistic vernacular of *The Great Dictator*, *Monsieur*

Verdoux, *Limelight*, and *A King in New York*, Chaplin moved from taking on segments of man's foibles to dealing with major issues and social values and political commentary. As might be expected, his audiences laughed less and less, and thought more and more. Psychologically, I suggest that through his films Chaplin was consistently, though partially, individuating from his core identification with the playful, illusory, and psychotically tinged magical world of his early mother and moving toward a new identificatory amalgam, consisting of the unreceptively grandiose and bitter world of his late mother combined with the cynically disappointing but more rational experience of his father. An oedipal winner and loser, Chaplin's victory was to remain vacuous, while his loss would remain profound. Unable to sufficiently idealize his competitor, Chaplin would be left with idealizing his own self, albeit in relatively functional ways. His competitive victory over his father was quite significant in the real world, but perhaps a bit shallow in his emotional world. His developmental movement was characterized by not only vastly outdoing his father's theatrical popularity, but by a successful though transference-based marriage to a rational and devoted self -object mother represented by Oona O'Neill, a new and much healthier edition of Chaplin's mother, as well as maintaining a healthier relationship with her than his parents had with each other.[10] Oona would serve both his developmental and regressed needs well. It seems to me that Chaplin the person was indeed able to work through a number of internal-developmental crises through his life course. Chaplin the film star used his films as a literal "dream screen" whose narrative and images give us a context for

---

10 And, as previously noted, an Oedipal victory over Oona's father Eugene O'Neill, who hated Chaplin.

comprehending how these processes of internal change and developmental shifts evolved.

CHAPTER 4

Chaplin: His Identity as Man and Shadow

It has been my thesis that Chaplin's personal crises cast an influential shadow over the characters portrayed by his screen images. As his life course evolved, his screen characters similarly evolved through various life stages, crises, and transitions (Brok 1991a,b). His characters became containers through which Chaplin could projectively deal with his conflicts. His screen images were used as a nonverbal analyst, quietly and empathically accepting and processing (but not feeding back) his projective identifications. The screen served as a transitional "play space." The audience however, unlike an empathic analyst, could not contain Chaplin's split off/paradoxical parts, nor could they comfortably identify with his later film characters. In defense, they maintained a split, and kept Chaplin's communications within his screen images and Chaplin himself. Thus, many in his audience could not empathically relate to Chaplin's internal dilemmas as projected onto the screen. Nor should they have. Unlike analysts, their prime function is receptivity, entertainment, and productive self-reflection, and not helping the actor, director, or producer understand himself better (and Chaplin was all three). In effect, however, the audience reacted to Chaplin's later films as an analyst who could not use his countertransference and enter into the patient's play space. Metaphorical communication about Chaplin's life experience became embedded in a context of aversive reactivity, while the aversive reality as communicated by Chaplin through a focus on play/humor became denied or illusory, or defended against by being judged not relevant. In short, a significant segment of Chaplin's audience attempted to push Chaplin's projective identifications back into him.

Chaplin the man was easy to capture but hard to identify. The quintessential "man without a country," his identity seems to have solidified around iconoclastic belonging. Idiosyncratic and individualistic, he remained without a firm mother-country or fatherland. *It is not an accident that he wound up living in Switzerland.* One gets the feeling that the "place" where he felt most "at home" was within his own set of values and later within his mutual and transference-based self-object tie with Oona O'Neill, who dedicated her life to him. In her youth (she was 17, he was 53) Charlie re-found his youthful mother, while in her rebellious uniqueness, Oona found her father. (Eugene O'Neill),[11] a perfect oedipal interlock, buttressed by pre-oedipal needs and satisfactions. His stable, happy, and enduring later

---

11 Relevant here is that Eugene O'Neill apparently hated Chaplin. And Oona was quite the rebel, slipping out of her private school dormitory to hang out in Greenwich Village, etc.

life marriage to Oona is exemplified by these quotes from an interview in his seventieth year (Robinson, 1985. p. 185):

In the sixteen years of our marriage, we have been separated only once – for five days (sic) when Oona went on a business trip to America. She is my inspiration, and she is a good critic. To get her reactions to anything I do, I let her see my day's output of work…She never discusses anything or proffers an opinion unless I ask her. Sometimes I disagree with her opinion only to find a week later that she was right.

We have profound respect for each other's taste and views, and this makes for a most agreeable atmosphere in the home. We can be thoroughly relaxed with each other and enjoy our own company without having to indulge in conversation. Oona feels that she has no talents, except as a wife and mother (Robinson 1985, pp. 595-96).

The remarkable consistency over time of their relationship is illustrated by comparing observations of the quality of Chaplin's experience with Oona at the beginning of their enduring love affair with the aforementioned description offered by "Charlie" some seventeen years later. Thus, Charles Junior, his son from a previous marriage, describes what he and his brother observed of their father and Oona early on:

Whenever Oona was with our father, a rapt expression would come into her eyes. She would sit quietly, hanging on his every word. Most women are charmed by Dad, but in Oona's case it was different. She worshipped him, drinking in every word he spoke, whether it was about his latest script, the weather or some bit of philosophy. She seldom spoke, but every now and then she would come up with one of those penetrating remarks that impressed even our father with her insight. (Robinson 1985. P.519)

Below is a photo of Charlie and Oona around the time they had just married.

Picture 23. Copyright Museum of Modern Art

Some Further Comments on Chaplin "The Man" – A Brief Early History

A fuller and more profound understanding of Chaplin can be derived from his autobiography. Here I will present a brief summary perspective on Chaplin's early history.

A brief review of Chaplin's early life yields a devastating picture. Born into poverty and abandoned by his father, young Charles grew up in wretched circumstances. By age ten he had been moved and uprooted countless times and been placed in special schools for destitute children when his mother was hospitalized for psychosis.[12] He learned to live by his wits in the streets of London. Some quotes from his autobiography give us a sense of his childhood and especially his mother.

I was hardly aware of my father, and do not remember his having lived with us. He died of alcoholic excess at age thirt-seven. They would tell stories about him with humor and sadness. He had a violent temper drinking and during one of his tantrums she (my mother) ran off to Brighton with some friends, and in answer to his frantic telegrams: "What are you up to?" She wired back: Balls, parties and picnics, darling. (Chaplin 1964, p.18)

At eighteen mother eloped with a middle-aged man to Africa. She often spoke of her life there, living in luxury amidst plantations, servants and saddle horses. In her eighteenth year my (older) brother Sydney was

---

12 Reportedly due to syphilis (Weisman, 2009).

born. I was told he was the son of a lord and would inherit a fortune at age twenty – information that both pleased and annoyed me.

Mother did not stay long in Africa but returned to England and married my father. I had no knowledge of what ended the African episode, but in our extreme poverty, I would reproach her for giving up such a wonderful life. She would laugh and say that she was too young to be cautious or wise. What degree of feeling she had for my father I never knew. Sometimes she would give a sympathetic account of him, at other times talk of his drunkenness and violence. In later years, whenever angry with me she would ruefully say, "You'll finish up in the gutter like your father." (Chaplin, 1964)

It is of interest that in many films, Chaplin, the shadow, would act (or come close to acting) his mother's prophecy out, while in real life, Chaplin, the man, was quite a successful capitalist.[13]

Chaplin's ongoing internal conflict about being "down and out" versus "cheerful and successful" was an underlying theme in his early films and in more subtle ways in his later, non-little tramp cinematic works.

Also of interest is another anecdote from Chaplin's autobiography concerning his mother:

---

13 Some examples are his selling all his stocks before the market crash in 1929, his friendship with the Hearst family, and his creation of United Artists with Douglas Fairbanks, Mary Pickford, and D. W. Griffith. And his signing a $670,000 contract in 1916 with the Mutual Film Corporation, a contract that is estimated at around ten million dollars in today's values.

Winter was approaching and Sydney ran out of clothes, so mother made him a coat from her old velvet jacket. It had red and blac striped sleeves, pleated at the shoulders, which mother did her best to get rid of, but with little success. Sydney wept when he was made to wear it. "What will the boys at school think?" "Who cares what people think," she said, "It looks very distinguished." Mother had such a persuasive way that Sydney to this day has never understood why he ever submitted to wearing it. But he did, and the coat and a pair of mother's cut down high heeled shoes got him into a figh at school. The boys called him, "joseph and his coat of many colors" and I, with a pair of red tights cut down for stockings, which looked as if they were pleated, was called, "Sir Francis Drake." (Chaplin, 1964)

Chaplin's mother had been an occasional stage actress, and seems to have communicated an appreciation of fantasy, playfulness, and illusion to her young son. Unfortunately, she was often lost in her fantasy, and would become quite dysfunctional; leaving her young sons to fend for themselves. One anecdote is illustrative of this woman's impact on young Charlie.

She would tell anecdotes and act them out, recounting an episode in the life of Emperor Napoleon: tip-toeing in his library to reach for a book, and being intercepted by Marshal Ney (Mother playing both characters; but always with humor. "Sirs, allow me to get it for you…

I am higher" and Napoleon with an indignant scowl saying: Higher? Taller!" In that dark room in the basement, mother illuminated to me the kindliest light this world had ever known, which has endowed literature and the theatre with their greatest and richest themes: love, pity and humanity. (Chaplin 1964. pp. 24-25).

One final anecdote describing Chaplin's relationship with his mother is contributed by Chaplin's now grown daughter Geraldine. Here she describes her father's capacity for disavowing the illness of his mother:

He always attributed his mother's illness to malnutrition, and not schizophrenia that I (Geraldine) suspect it was. Charlie's memories of his mother were not all unhappy. She sometimes reduced him to tears of mirth by inventing stories about the people they could see through windows. Chaplin would also amuse Geraldine with tales of the eccentricities of Hannah's (his mother) later years after he brought her to safety in America. She would get very worried for instance, if she saw an open manhole, fearing the men inside were getting dangerously hot. If she could, she would buy an ice cream cone and dump it on any head that emerged saying "cool down, cool down." On a visit to a California ostrich farm, she picked up an egg waiting to be hatched and broke it with a solicitous cry of "poor thing, it'll need it's mother." Her last words were to ask the nurses to remove the glass of water beside her bed. "Those poor fish," she said, "take them out, they are going to drown." Chaplin would chuckle at such memories, but not without sadness. (Interview,[14] *New York Times*, March 22, 1992, p 16)

---

14 Weismann (2009) notes that Chaplin's mother suffered from syphilis. Whatever her ultimate diagnosis, she exhibited bizarre behavior at times.

Perhaps one of the best observations of Chaplin, the man, is given by Thomas Burke, a writer who knew the early Chaplin and his context well. Burke, in a brilliant essay written at the height of Chaplin's fame, captures much of what may be helpful to our understanding. Robinson (1985) gives considerable space to this essay which was written in 1935. Burke came from the same time period, social background, and part of London as Chaplin. He and Chaplin came to know each other in 1921. They kept up a steady acquaintance over the next decade. Burke seems to have deeply understood Charlie's inner voice. Robinson writes: "Burke loved Chaplin without idolatry, he called him this hard, bright, icy creature and understood him perhaps better than any other man in his lifetime." Robinson goes on to note that "Burke's essay is essential to the discovery of Chaplin." Robinson (1985, p. 443). In this light, let us look at some excerpts:

A man of querulous outlook, self centred, moody, and vaguely dissatisfied with life. That is the kind of man he is, or nearly. For to get to him is not easy. It is impossible to see him straight. He dazzles everybody – the intellectual, the simple, the cunning, and even those who meet him every day. At no stage can one make a fine sketch and say: "This is Charles Chaplin, " Wasn't it?" He's like a brilliant, flashing now from this facet and now from that – blue, green yellow, crimson by turns. A brilliant is the apt simile: he's hard and bright as that, and his lustre is as erratic. If you split him you would find, as with the brilliant, and as with Charles Dickens, that there was no personal source of those charging lights; they were only the flashings of genius. It is almost impossible to locate him, I doubt he can locate himself."

As Robinson notes, Burke does attempt to "locate Chaplin":

"He is often as kind and tender as any man could be, but often inconsiderate. He shrinks from the limelight, but misses it if it isn't turned upon him. He is intensely shy, yet loves to be the centre of attention. A born solitary, he knows the fascination of the crowd. He is really and truly modest, but very much aware that there is nobody quite like Charles Chaplin. He expects to get his own way in everything and usually gets it. Life hampers him, he wants wings. He wants to eat his cake and have it. He wants peau de chagrin for granting of all his wishes, but the peau de chagrin must not diminish. He makes excessive demands upon life and upon people, and because these demands cannot always be answered, he is perplexed and irritated. He commands the loyalty of his friends, while being casual himself. He takes their continuing friendship for granted. He likes the best of the current social system, while at heart he is the reddest of Reds. Full of impulsive generosities he is also capable of the opposite. He takes himself seriously, but has a sharp sense of humor about himself and his doings. He has a genuine humility about the position he has won, but, like most other humble artists, he doesn't always like you to take the humility as justified. For hours he will be the sweetest fellow you have ever sat with; then, without apparent cause, he will be all petulance and asperity. Like a child, his interest is quickly caught and he is quickly bored. In essence he is still a Cockney, but he is no longer English – if he ever was. In moments of excitement, and in all his work, the Cockney appears. At other times, he is, in manners, speech and attitude, American. He is

not at all in sympathy with the reserved English character, and he feels little for England and English things.

He is one of the most honest of men. If you ask his opinion on anything or anybody you get it a straight and clear. Most of us have some touch of humbug about us, but Charles has none. You can accept anything he says for the truth as he sees it. A point of his honesty is his selfishness. Most of us are selfish, in one way or another, but are annoyed if people bring the accusation. Yet selfish people are usually more agreeable by pleasing themselves they maintain a cheerful demeanor to those about them. Charles lives as most of us would if we had the necessary nerve to face ourselves as we really are however disturbing the "reality" might be to our self-esteem.

He will only do wants to do. If an engagement is in opposition to the mood of the moment, he breaks it, and if asked why he didn't keep it he will blandly answer – Because he didn't want to. In whatever company he might be, he is simple and spontaneous. He may be always living in a part, but he never poses; has a hatred of sham.

His life at home, despite the Japanese valets and cooks and chauffeurs, is not the glamorous crowded affair that some people imagine it to be. He told me that he leads almost a humdrum a life as a London clerk. He is not overly popular in that lunatic asylum, one could hardly expect Hollywood to know what to make of a poet – and they leave him pretty much to himself. His mind is extraordinarily quick and receptive; retentive too. He reads very little, but with a few elementary facts on a highly technical subject, his mind can so work upon them that he can talk with an expert on that subject in such a way as to make the expert think. He thus appears a very well read and cultivated man, when in fact his acquaintance with books is slight. With little interest in people, he yet has a swifter eye than any novelist I know for oddities and their carefully hidden secrets. It is useless to pose before him, he can call your bluff in the moment of being introduced. He is now (1931) forty-two in years, but he cannot live up to that age, and never will. His attitude and interest are always towards youth and younger things. He takes no concern in the historical past; his spiritual home is his own period. He is intensely a child of these times and his mind finds nothing to engage it further back than his own boyhood. "I always feel like such a kid," he told me once, "among grown-ups." (Burke 1931. in Robinson 1985, pp. 443–445)

CHAPTER 5

The Aesthetic Therapeutic Contract: Understanding the Patient's Self and Shadow

Clinical Listening and the "Playing Alliance"

My earlier discussion about play (Chapter 2) suggests that play in the therapeutic session involves listening to the patient without active involvement in theory. Theory is there in the background, but not in the foreground. We listen to our patient, to his experience, and see what emerges in both of us. Analyst and patient open themselves to the potential space within the session. Under these conditions, both are at play. The material that emerges is then matched to the background theory available to the analyst. Here the theoretical repertoire of the analyst becomes important. The analyst does not fit the patient's material directly into his pre-set notions; he first experiences the material with the patient, senses his own associations, and then feels a sense of emergence from his palette of theories, life experiences, and experience and knowledge of his patient gained through the session events to date. What denotes the playing alliance then is that the analyst is attending to his internal free associations to the patients material while in a state of free-floating attention. We are not organizing our patient's data, we are letting ourselves be organized by the data. In essence we are not allowing the patient's "shadow" to darken the breadth of our associations. For I am suggesting that when we allow a patient's content to prematurely narrow the scope and divergent quality of our internal associations, as when conflict or anxiety is set up within us, and our resultant constriction pushes us away from a sense of "free play" in the moment, thereby stifling the internal emergence of a truly empathic sense of the patient's self; we become entangled in the patient's shadow and we lose the comprehension of the source (much as Chaplin's audience got entangled in Chaplin's shadow). Similar to an audience which abrogates its aesthetic contract with an artist, we abrogate our aesthetic therapeutic contract with a patient we no longer follow. Instead of searching for discovery and understanding, we may rely on rapid finding and interpretation. What denotes the working alliance is the patient's observing reality ego in collaboration with the analyst's analyzing ego. I am suggesting the working alliance may depend upon the prior establishment of a playing alliance. In sum, we ask not what the patient means, but what experience does his content bring to both of us. We are not actively searching for meaning, we are more passively scanning *our* experience *and* our experience *of the patient* over time, for what we can discover. We are not searching or looking for something we can find, as much as what we may *discover*. This presumes a trust in our comfort with our own spontaneous associative process in the moment. It also assumes an expanded repertoire of ways of being that are "*comfortable*" for the analyst.

One example of an analyst missing the "playing alliance" can be seen in a case described by Modell (1990, p. 55). He describes a situation where he takes the patient literally rather than metaphorically.

Modell reports the patient as asking him, "Are you bored," during a session in which she is withdrawn and silent. Modell responds with a self-disclosure, saying "Yes, I was bored," and goes on to reassure her that "my boredom was not a rejection of her but a response to her withdrawal, etc." The patient responds angrily and feels rejected. Modell goes on to describe the justification for his response:

> *Previously I had sidestepped such questions, but I now felt that our relationship was sufficiently secure that I could respond to her question in a more direct fashion. After telling her yes, I I was bored, I said further that I knew this to be something that she needed to do; I wished to convey to her that I was not being critical of the fact that she was withdrawn, but was trying to understand why she needed to do so at this particular time.*[15]

---

15 So I wonder how could he be bored if he was thinking about what was going on or free associating to his experience of her state of being. It would seem he was not in such a place, but, rather, needing to be entertained by her. And his subsequent explanation for his disclosure reveals that he was finding, rather than discovering, what was going on. His repertoire of possibility in this instance was quite narrow. His assumption reveals that he wasn't "playing" with various possibilities.

Modell goes on:

"It should be noted that this patient had read some of my publications on the subject of boredom as a countertransference response. Thus there was something collegial in my response, which proved to be a misjudgment, in that I mistakenly judged the patient to in a more mature position than she actually was. This error in clinical judgement no doubt represented a wish: my collegial response was experienced as a rejection of her; she felt that I did not understand that I was out of synchrony with her.

The point here is that Modell more playfully might have responded with "your question interests me, I'm not bored (implying you don't need to entertain me) – I am an interested audience to you but I am experiencing your silence with the assumption that you are conveying something to me, but I am not sure what." Or, "I've been thinking about it and wondering why you need to apparently withdraw at this particular time? Can you help me with this? What are you experiencing in my presence today? Perhaps we are both avoiding something?" If Modell had merely asked, "What do you think?", he, of course, would be moving away from the "playing alliance," as I define it.

My suggested intervention I think illustrates a relational approach and the closeness of such an approach to my notion of the "playing alliance" (Brok 1991b). Modell admits his mistake, I would say, due to his treating the situation literally. I see this as an example of his having a restricted repertoire or "palette of theories/ responses" at that moment, due to his restriction in the breadth (divergent thinking capacity) of his internal free associations in this particular therapeutic moment. This in turn might have been due to his "cognitive awareness" of a need to narcissistically believe the patient was interested in him (his article on boredom) rather than to free associate to the patient's subjective experience in the moment about their relationship. What I am arguing is that the rational concept of time and reality crept in to the therapy at the moment the patient was relating to the therapist in the here and now. So, it seems, Modell was not at the moment being empathic, but rather he was being interpretive. Simply put, he privileged finding the rational rather than looking at discovering what the patient experience might be about through the patient's associations and/or his own associations.

Even within his narrow repertoire, Modell might have more productively used his inner experience, by sharing with the patient his actual assumption, with the added advisement such as *"I am not bored, I'm wondering if you are thinking about my article on boredom, at least that's what's come into my mind when I was experiencing your silence."* Instead Modell shared his interpretation but not his associations! This abrogated the possibility of discovering if the patient's associations validated his (Modell's) assumptions. Here we see the issue of the analyst organizing the patient as opposed to being organized by the patient. For Modell, theory/assumption was in the foreground rather than the background. In my opinion, this is an example of the analyst short-circuiting the "playing alliance" by moving too quickly into a working alliance mode.

The achievement of a working alliance with some patients may depend upon the experience of a mutually enjoyed playing alliance The playing alliance depends upon the patient's sense of the analyst's involvement with his experience in a manner that can be emotionally understood, i.e the quality is direct; and the experience encompasses more than just the previous session's events. It is in this sense that the "playing alliance" has a similarity to the emphasis developmentally- oriented theorists and researchers, such as Stern (1985) place on the importance of "emotional attunement" or "affective fitting" between patient and analyst. I might also note that clinicians such as the Sandlers (1978) have also stressed that the analyst's emotional responsiveness may be put forward as the crucial working tool alongside "evenly hovering attention." Likewise Sandler and Sandler (1978) have highlighted the importance of the analyst's "free-floating responsiveness" in addition to free-floating attention.[16] Others who talk of play in the clinical setting such as Ehrenberg (1990) note that:

Working playfully requires spontaneity and often means trusting one's intuitive clinical sensibility before it can be consciously thought through. Although it is not calculated or premeditated, this does not mean it is thoughtless, and not derivative of one's clinical expertise. On the contrary, even decisions to be playful sometimes may precede rather than follow more conscious kinds of logical consideration, that involves complex clinical judgments. The question becomes do we think a particular response will be technically facilitating, rather than do we understand exactly what is going on with the patient, the treatment or ourselves, at any given moment. Heimann's (1950)

---

[16] I must say that this is quite connected to a sense of "mutually involved witnessing between patients and analyst." (Brok 1991)

observation that the analyst's unconscious is always ahead of his or her conscious in relation to the patient seems relevant. I think it is this level of our own experience that we actually draw upon when we make a decision to intervene playfully or not. (Ehrenberg, 1990, pp. 77–78)

Although I agree with Ehrenberg's basic notion, I disagree with her stress on not needing to understand what is going on with the patient. I think we *come* to understand and it is this which informs our response.

Trauma, Play, and Impingement in the Clinical Session

It is clear that we are vulnerable to trauma from the start of our existence and that trauma, as experienced in infancy, is the most psychically impactful. Though the literature is replete with concepts of "psychological trauma" versus "real trauma," "cumulative trauma," "strain trauma," "shock trauma," and with discussion of differences in dealing with trauma at different life stages, I shall in this work deal with impingements on early mother-child involvement and then "father loss" trauma. In light of the above, Fromm (1989), following a Winnicottian perspective, suggests that:

Defensive operations are early on directed against impingements which lead to an overly intense reaction in the infant and hence fragment his developing sense of continuity. Winnicott refers to these early traumatic experiences as "primitive agonies" (1974) in response to which withdrawal dissociation, disintegration and depersonalization are early efforts at self-

preservation. (I would add primitive thought.) Winnicott's accent here is on a danger situation of a very special sort; dangers that are less localized and differentiated than castration or separation anxiety and that threaten the rudimentary self with its total annihilation. Defenses come into play in response to the trauma of overwhelming affective states, rather than as would be the case later in development; such as dealing with forbidden impulses (my thought here is that early defensive operations prevent the fruition of play states, which require a non-defensive illusion space). The false self organization would be the paradigmatic defensive operation from a Winnicottian point of view, in that it is geared toward the maintenance of a relationship with the impinging but needed other through compliance, while also preserving in a dissociated way, in a weakened but inviolate condition, some core of true self functioning. (Fromm 1989, p.7)

It has been my clinical observation, that patients who have had a developmental history marked by "premature" impingements tend to escape into a pseudo (too rapid) working alliance when a nascent playing alliance has been disrupted by some serious experience – near difficult therapeutic event.

The point that I am making is that a "play state" needs to be achieved by the patient with the analyst, in order for the analytic work to proceed. The development and safeguarding of this affective mutually created relation between patient and analyst becomes the crucial therapeutic task, especially for patients with a pseudo or false self characterological organization. I think that Winnicott would of course agree with such a perspective. His theory includes an exquisite appreciation of the fact that things happen to the infant before the infant, as a separate being, is there for things to happen to it. At the pre-awareness level of experience, the sense of organismic-system developmental safety and its metaphoric analogue, basic trust, are very much an ongoing operation. The balance is delicate and impingements, i.e. traumas, have their shunting effects. One such shunting effect is toward the rational; the other, as I have previously mentioned, is toward the extremely illusional.

Clinical Example; The Less Integrated Patient

Thomas, a thirty-three year old male analysand in his 18 month of a four time a week treatment had been slowly and incrementally allowing himself to:

1. Look at me when he left the office and say good-bye.
2. Smile in greeting rather than keeping a bland sometimes scowling face.
3. Occasionally make what he termed "small talk" and playfully tell me a "silly joke."
4. Tell me he felt my voice as sincere.
5. Free associate with a diminished need to keep attentive to any minute sound or shift in position on my part.
6. To directly share his experience of me without prefacing it with an apology.
7. Become less conscious of time during the session (For a while he would look at his wristwatch every few minutes, in order to not "run over.")
8. To associate to his dreams rather than analyze them for me to "understand."
9. React with emotion to my experience of him, rather than tell me what he thought his emotion meant.
10. To share his fantasies of me as well as with me.

In short, we had entered a sense of mutuality of experience quite different from the sense of "compliance with the treatment" I initially experienced with him. At this juncture, our sessions were becoming more steeped in the play-like quality of a shame-free unguarded experience. An experience of closeness and unity, long defended against by this patient, was slowly evolving. In this sense, Thomas was allowing himself to be located by me. A guest in his psychic house, I felt like an anthropologist being accepted into the local community. I was living in his territory, which he had expanded to include and create me, rather than expecting him to live in mine.[17] And we were both discovering previously hidden blocked and frozen inner resources that he had tucked away and, through our work, were incrementally melting.

As we know, however, analysis does not proceed in a straight incremental line. Due to a traffic problem, I arrived some 20 minutes late for one of our \sessions. This impinging fact severely broke the experience of unity, and along with it my patient's sense of safety for play/illusion. Fantasy gave way to awareness and a need to consider my reasons for not being there and its impact on him. (The alternative would have been to deny the experience, which he did not do.) The illusion that I was at least partly his creation, which I had struggled to encourage by being a consistent presence, had been shattered by the momentousness of my absence as he struggled for the rest of the session to maintain a "playing alliance" via appealing to the working alliance. Thus, to quote:(Talking to himself) *Dr Brok is not usually late… this must have been unusual… No. something is weird… I don't know*

---

17 Just as Chaplin tries to re-locate his "kid" in *A King in New Yor,k* i.e. by his quote in the scene with the young idealistic kid," You think too much, you should play more." Thomas and I had managed to temporarily furlough the rational world of solely analyzing for the bounded and safe space of "playing."

what to think...let me concentrate... almost walked out (but) said no...this is what Bonnie (former girlfriend) did to me and I didn't like it, and now I have to think about it....I don't feel good. Oh... Oh... moans.

In this session, the intrusive element of stark reality, rather than the background field reality forces the shift from the conflict-free illusion-safe sphere, to the conflict necessary, illusion-and-play unsafe sphere. Even though I apologized for being late, myself frustrated with the traffic delay, he nevertheless had to *think,* and we could indeed analyze his reaction in relation to the reality and the context of the steadiness of treatment and his transference fantasies. He was forced to think about how he organized his experience, rather than experience it. Impingement necessitates organization to deal with it, which in turn can necessitate false self structuralization. My patient was eventually able to "re-play," after all, we did have a history together; but it took a while to re-locate him and for him to find me. Luckily, it was like an intermission between acts in a theater, rather than a play one walks out of.

Play and Trust

It is my belief that one cannot truly play if one cannot truly trust; and one cannot easily trust if one has been traumatized early on. So for many of our patients, as with Thomas, the main therapeutic task remains helping them play again. It may be that play develops co-equivalently with trust. Their point of origin may differ, but their qualities are isomorphic. As Fromm (1989, p. 14) notes, for example, both Winnicott and Erikson :

elevate the concept of play to a new level of importance as the basic medium of evolving integration. Winnicott's discussion of illusion, which eventually takes shape as the transitional object, has to do with the earliest forms of play; the outcome of good -enough mothering during the transitional phase is the child's fundamental confidence in his capacity to create and/or find in the world that which he needs; a strength akin to Erikson's concept of basic trust, but accented more from the inside. (Fromm 1989. p 14)

Play, it would seem, is dependent on the total experiential field. As an internal state dependent on the system in which it is embedded, the experience "play-trust" is clearly an ecological notion. In this respect, it seems that to fully understand the ramifications of this state we need to develop a science of play, perhaps built on ideas developed by social psychologists such as Barker (1964) and his concept of behavior setting theory but integrated with an intra-psychic relational perspective. Play, as all human states, is located within a context!

Trauma and Trust

If trauma disrupts the self-experience, it also greatly disrupts the interpersonal sense of trust, creating a sense of dislocation of self *in* relation to the environmental context *in* which the self is located. *In short, trauma disconnects.*In this light, I may say that we need a Context-Relations theory to complement Object-Relations theories, since disconnection tends to involve dislocation. Dislocation inevitably results in the loss of what I term "Linking Assumptions," which is the psychic structure that helps us feel located *in* the world. For example, it has long been known that if geriatric patients are moved from one nursing home to another without adequate preparation, they may experience extreme disruption of their sense of location. The ensuing sequelae such as depression, disorganization, and death can be traced to the enormous sense of dislocation and concomitant break in their sense of linkage to the environment.[18] (Weiner, Brok and Snadowsky, 1987). A linking assumption is a self and location connection. When such a connection is severed, as it is by some forms of trauma, we are left to existentially float – a core with no safe context. The loss of this safe context, and its resultant sense as a persecutory context, becomes a source of a new identification: identification with the traumatic context, or as I have put it "traumatic identification" (Brok 2006). This identification in turn becomes a basic experiential state. In effect, one becomes one's context.

In light of the above, it is relevant to note that at least one writer on trauma has suggested:

> *The damage to relational life is not a secondary effect of trauma, as originally thought. Traumatic events have primary effects not only on psychological structures of the self but also on the systems of attachment and meaning that link individual and community. (Berman 1992. P. 51)*

A break in linking assumption can also lead to a sort of foreclosed solution such as "existential identification." Sartre, for example, who suffered, and

---

18 A linking assumption is roughly analogous to trust, but an ecological trust, as well as an interpersonal trust. It is also related to issues of attachment.

denied, the affective impact of the permanent dislocation trauma of the loss of his father at age fifteen months, was to comment, "*The death of my father was the greatest piece of good fortune. I didn't even have to forget him.*" (Hayman 1987, p. 31). Except, as I suggest, his memory lived on in Sartre's detached existential philosophy! Chaplin too, I am arguing, used the dislocating experiences of his youth and the loss of his father to espouse a rather bitter and cynical philosophy which he expressed and worked on dealing with in his later films – as his idealization of human capacity for equality and empathy broke down.[19] Although Chaplin attempted to work out many of his personal life conflicts and issues via his films, he could never locate himself in a homeland.It is not an accident that Chaplin finally located himself in "neutral" Switzerland. He never returned to live in England, nor did he become a citizen of the United States though he lived and worked in the U.S. for over 50 years.[20]

---

19 We should note that in two of his films, one silent (*The Kid*) and the other a talkie (*A King in New York*), we can see attempts to be fatherly to a dislocated aspect of himself.

20 There are some remarkable similarities between Chaplin and Sartre. However, there are also major differences. Chaplin, for example, was able much more able to sustain a committed object-relation, though skewed in the direction of his needing a partner who would be a self-object rather than an equal. He also had and desired children. Sartre's relation with Simone De Beauvoir was much more distant.

CHAPTER 6

Play and Humor

I think that play can be experienced without humor, but that the attitude of humor requires a prior sense of playfulness. When this does not happen without a prior sense of playfulness, it becomes "crisp" and sarcastic, a function of the superego, rather than built on the elevating and somewhat narcissistic pleasurable base of the ego ideal. Simply put, I believe play is a non-conative state; there is no intentionality in play, only the cognitive and affective experience. This is in keeping with my thesis that play is nonverbal at its base.[21] Play is a state of being which might have positive consequences for one's development, as well as positive consequences for one's relationship with a reciprocating and involved 'other," but it is entered into as a way of simply being in the process/moment.

---

21 Of interest: the nonverbal base of play, in a discussion by Yerushalmi, in which he compared the verbal-conative qualities of Freud with the nonverbal element in Schoenberg. One became an analyst, the other a composer. (Yerushalmi 1992).

Humor is reflective, conative, and often defensive. It is *intended* to express a state of being and/or sometimes defend against an anxious or feared state of experience. *Life is paradoxical, things are not always serious, we are not perfect, I am absurd, but not ashamed. I am triumphant over depression, etc.* Humor is verbal and social. Humor can also be a way of overcoming trauma, rather than the experiencing of trauma. Humor is in the domain of later development. Children play, then joke, and develop humor along with superego development.

Freud also relates humor to qualities kindred to joy and based in narcissism. Humor, he notes, procures a feeling of elation for the ego, as opposed to melancholia where the ego is crushed.

> *The grandeur in it clearly lies in the triumph of the narcissistic, the victorious assertion of the ego's invulnerability. The ego refuses to be distressed by the provocations of reality to let itself be compelled to suffer. It insists that it cannot be affected by the traumas of the external world… Humor is not resigned, it is rebellious. (Freud 1927, pp. 162–163)*

In effect, the pleasure principle has been idealized, it has become *an* ego ideal; a quality of experience to which one aspires, (as it implies a goal orientation aspiration). In effect, it becomes a conative rather than non-conative process, even if we stay within Freud's system. Humor, then, accepts reality but triumphs over it through a combination of defensive dynamics and illusional ideals. It is a meeting point for superego and ego ideal. Humor occurs (is located) at the intersection of superego and ego ideal. Just where this "intersection" occurs is important. Thus, I am suggesting that humor which is short on idealization of the instinct and long on superego formation becomes cruel and primarily an outlet for the expression of aggression, sadism, and sarcasm. When projected it becomes paranoid/persecutory. When humor is long on idealization of the instinct (i.e. ego ideal) and short on superego formation, it becomes illusional/delusional and hard to comprehend. Both forms of humor in the extreme are experienced as "not funny."

Within Freud's energetic framework; the superego has a special role in humor. In particular, he suggests that the humorous attitude involves the withdrawal of cathexis from the ego and transposing it onto the superego. As noted by Chasseguet-Smirgel (1988, p.199):

To the superego thus inflated, the ego can appear tiny and all its interests trivial. Humor would... (then) be the contribution made by the comic through the agency of the super-ego. (Of interest here is the concept of the super-ego as a protective agency, given to distortion of reality by abetting the sense of illusion.)... as if it were saying to the ego, "look!" here is the world which seems so dangerous! It is nothing but a game for children – just worth making a jest of. (Freud 1927, pp. 164–166, also in Chasseguet-Smirgel 1988, p. 199.)[22]

It might be said that the process for humor is quite similar to the defensive style of a manic state. Humor however evokes a human softness and

---

[22] As alluded to previously, it is a clear dynamic portrayed in the award-winning film *Life Is Beautiful* (1997).

poignancy that mania does not. I think part of that softness involves an acceptance of the absurd. Which I daresay is a mature aspect of humor?

It is in keeping with my thesis that Chaplin was moving in this direction as he went from silent films to "talkies" – only to find his humor (being embedded in serious reality/political social issues) becoming too cynical for some audiences, which in turn dwarfed for some whatever play/comic/ maturely absurd elements could be found in his later films. It is also my thesis that Chaplin the man was attempting to resolve internal conflicts via Chaplin the "shadow" as it was reflected on the film dream screen.

As humor leads with superego-functions from above and narcissistic and/or oral and anal disappointments from below, sarcasm, judgmentalism, criticism, moralism, sadism, and punitive themes emerge as messages to others in the form of jokes. From this perspective we can see that Chaplin's role in losing some of his audience was due to his tendency to hold on to "incongruous to the situation" play and humor, as he developed a biting, sometimes sarcastic, and critical part of himself which he projected into his screen persona.

In Chaplin's later films, sequences which might be considered playful and humorous if they were independent of any serious content became hard to emotionally handle as such, when they were embedded in the thematic ecology of the film narrative. These sequences are not "comic relief" as much as tragic attempts to maintain levity (in a manic style?) in depressing circumstances. For example, when the now quite aged Chaplin attempts a slapstick routine, the kind that was so successful in his early films, in his next to last major film *A King in New York* (1957) it simply looks sad and absurd in light of the overall theme of the film which is a critique of the House Un–American Activities Committee, nuclear weapons, and American culture.

Further Thoughts on the Origin of Humor

In humor, the illusion of well-being is not complete; depressive content often seeps through – but is not "given into." There remains a triumphant quality of the human spirit. In play, the illusion of well-being is complete, but not to the point of an enduring delusional state. Time and the rational are not avoided; they are simply not important at the moment. We live in our play, partially denying our experience in our humor. ***Play is a state of being; humor can be used to reflect on our state of being.***

Play then seems to be related to what I term "momentary joy," and humor may be related to "joie de vivre." a pervasive sense that life is worth enjoying despite its depressing or tragic qualities. Chasseguet-Smirgel notes that humor generally brings a smile, not laughter, and moves one to admiration of the humorist's narcissistic triumph, his rebellion against exterior reality. She goes on to remind us that, as early as 1905, Freud noted that humor may only partly succeed in stopping the production of painful affect; this is the humor that smiles through tears (p. 232). And yet, despite this, the victory by humor is no less complete. "*On the contrary, the more one is aware of the tragedy of the situation the more humor takes a sublime turn.*" *(Chasseguet-Smirgel 1988, p. 202)*

Chasseguet-Smirgel (1988) goes on to suggest that the moment the humorist produces humor, he is protecting himself against the loss of love. While play is related to "momentary joy," can humor be related to the notion of "joie-de-vivre" which I proposed earlier on? The particular way that the serious and funny are joined together in humor is an important indicator of a life-affirming attitude. The Italian analyst Pasquali, in a survey of humor in psychoanalysis, notes that Freud felt humor to be the "*highest expression of the adaptive mechanisms, because it succeeds in restraining the compulsion to make a choice, between suffering and denial.* She also notes that in the analytic situation, *it affords the opportunity to face and work out the causes for the suffering.*" (Pasquali, 1987, p. 234)

The Mother and Humor: Some Speculations:

…not everyone is capable of the humorous attitude. . It is a rare and precious gift, and many people are even without the capacity to enjoy humorous pleasure that is presented to them. And finally, if the superego tries by means of humour to console the ego and prevent it from suffering, this does not contradict its origin in the parental agency. (Freud 1927. p. 166)

But just who is the embodiment of this parental agency? Is it the Oedipal parent or the pre-oedipal mother? Freud's response within the structural theory is that the ego is divided into an adult part, identified with the super – ego , and a part that plays the role of the child being consoled by the well-wishing superego, this consolation being accompanied by a shift in cathexis from the ego onto the superego. This new distribution of energy between the agencies, the hypercathexis of the superego to the detriment of the ego, allows the superego to suppress or alter the ego's reactions. In humor, "*the*

Superego is actually repudiating reality and serving an illusion. (Chasseguet-Smirgel 1988, pp. 200–201)

"*It is the mother who consoles the child, taking it in her arms and saying "it's nothing", you'll be better soon, or who blows on a hurt to make the pain disappear, not the oedipal father on whom the Freudian superego is founded.*" (Chasseguet-Smirgel 1988, p. 205). It is a precocious lack of maternal care that explains the relation of humor to depression. *The humorist is a person trying to **be** his own loving mother, the "good enough mother" he has not known and who assures the child in a state of deriliction, that he still is, who pretends, it's nothing, you'll be better soon." But this loving mother has never been truly assimilated into the ego." (Chasseguet Smirgel 1988, p. 205).* Presumably, this is what leads to the need for humor. The life attitude achieved by humor is a function of having had at least what Chasseguet-Smirgel calls a *"furtive glimpse" of what the "loving mother" might have been. Giving the young humorist to be his motives for prefiguring the satisfying narcissistic state – or a return it'* (Chasseguet-Smirgel 1988, p. 201–2).

My own clinical experience shows there may be some truth to this notion, though I also believe, based on clinical experience, that the attitudinal role of the father (or paternal proxy in later life) is crucial for developing a truer, non-cynical form of "joie-de-vivre" humor. For example, here is a patient who vividly recalled her "iodine" mother. Her mother, though loving at times, had many lapses of depression, sadism, and bizarre behavior. One example of which was her pattern of being a "friendly nurse" to the children on her block, always putting mercurochrome on their skinned knees, etc., while my patient, when hurt playing, was only giving iodine. Struggling to keep a sense of humor, my patient referred to this experience jokingly, but with great underlying sarcasm and cynicism. Her father, described as a difficult and negativistic man, had done little during her childhood years to assuage her anger, which later manifested through cynical humor. It was only through her marriage to a more fun-loving and whimsical man (compared with her father), and her experience in treatment with her male therapist (me) that enabled her to soften and develop a more full-hearted sense of playfully-based humor. This patient, who entered treatment with a considerable chip on her shoulder, terminated her combined individual and subsequent group treatment with a beautiful symbolic gesture. She brought in a rose to each member of her therapy group with the thorns removed to symbolize her changed internal attitude towards life and interpersonal feelings. She literally did not need to "prick" anyone, yet had not lost her ability to confront with appropriate anger and assertion.

It is intriguing to think that the above material on humor describes Chaplin's history with his mother and absent father. For example, to the extent that Chaplin's later films became less playful and even less humorous, perhaps because he no longer needed to be his "own loving mother" as he had his young wife, Oona, in this role. along with what amounted to an oedipal victory being a true father (let's not forget that he and Oona produced a bunch of children! Eight with Oona.) Thus by identifying with the Father role, and being a better father than his own, he might have become free to deal with and mourn the loss of his mother and move on to (or unearth) a more cynical sarcastic type of humor that didn't quite hit the mark with some audiences. On the "dream screen" of his later films, we see serious themes peppered with furtive moments of playfulness and cynical humor embedded in the stark reality which impinged all around him. This reflected the stark reality of Chaplin's perspective on the evils extant in capitalistic societies, in combination with the stark reality of Chaplin's early history in his familial and social ecology – in particular, the poverty and abandonment in which he lived. From this perspective, the social and political issues of his current time that he was commenting on, these were also metaphors for his mother's dysfunctional qualities and his abandoning yet cherished father's tragic parental attitude. Chaplin's humor, though embedded in the joy of "momentary play," never fully achieved "joie-de-vivre" humor devoid of cynicism and sarcasm, although he came awfully close!

Play, Humor, the Father in the Transference and the Use of an Actment: An Example with a Better Integrated Patient

Assistant Professor L. reluctantly came to analytic therapy after waiting some eight months after he was referred to me. The precipitating factor had been the sudden death of his father. This had left him ill at ease and sleepless. His mourning was foreclosed by denial and various forms of acting out. Beyond this tragic experience, he lacked any enthusiasm for academic activities necessary for his own personal growth and qualification for tenure at his university, an institution he vituperatively devalued. Adrift on a sea of life for many a decade; his history seemed to reveal a vaguely languished sense of depression marked by occasional spurts of ambition and fun-loving activities. He impressed me as kind, but somewhat unreachable. He eschewed virtually anything assertive or aggressive. His relationships with women seemed to be passive and masochistically tinged, Now at age 39, divorced for 17 years after a brief early marriage, he seemed to be moving in no particular direction.

Professor L. described his father as a "frustrated geologist" who could not go on to graduate school because when his father died, the family was left in poor economic circumstances. As a result, my patient's father supported his family for a number of years by becoming a civil servant and stayed in that position until his retirement.

Assistant Professor L. described his father as a "nice but meek man" who endured embarrassing public devaluations from his wife about his purported sexual incapacity.

In terms of his father's meekness, Assistant Prof. L. recalled how at age twelve he came home crying and angry after having been pushed around, kicked, and taunted by tough kids in the working-class neighborhood in which he lived – only to have his father say "don't make waves." Even though he was afraid, he recalled desperately wanting his father to either go out and yell at them and /or to encourage him to go out and fight and not take "that shit." He had been called a "dirty-Jew fag" by these kids. (The name calling had an additional complex meaning in that my patient's mother was a Catholic and his father Jewish.)

His father's reticent attitude toward encouraging a more spirited position by his son was further exemplified by the "newspaper route fiasco." As a youngster, my patient reported he was often too lazy to get himself up early to deliver newspapers on a short route he had during high school. His father, instead of waking his son to make sure they were delivered, went out himself to deliver the papers for his son.

Assistant Prof. L. had a lot going for him in a positive way. Though riddled with adolescent fears, he was lively, intellectual and not pretentious. Though filled with anxiety and conflicted about commitment, he was likeable. There was a Huckleberry Finn quality to him, and he probably would have been at home in a Mississippi river town in the 1880s. His father having kept geology as a hobby, used to take long treks in the hills with him looking for different rock formations. As a result, he felt comfortable with all sorts of wildlife, which was unconsciously used as an outlet for the expression of what I interpreted as phallic aggression and narcissism. For example, he collected snakes and tried to keep them secretly hidden under his bed. Occasionally, one would get loose and cause havoc with his mother who in turn would lash out uncontrollably towards her son, expecting her husband to further punish him. From his father he would get only a quiet reprimand. His mother's hysteria frightened him, his father's measured response actually disappointed him.

Assistant Prof. L.'s first year of treatment was marked by forgotten sessions which he would grandiosely expect me to make up (which I didn't) and much other testing of limits. He was intimidated by me, although unconsciously envious and competitive. Eventually he regressed (progressed?) to a position of idealizing me and at other times felt inhibited and shamed in my presence. Feelings of love and respect for important men began to emerge in his associations – the chairman of his department, people in his field who made a mark, fantasies about my success, and a deeper sense of what he wished his father to have been became important themes. (One important theme was his recognition of the conflicts and limitations his father must have felt, while avoiding conscious acceptance of his competitive desire to go beyond him.) As therapy progressed, his relations with women were becoming more assertive and less masochistic.

Specific Vignette

The vignette I am reporting took place towards the end of his second year of treatment. My office at the time was on the street level facing a large avenue. A short time into the session, a flurry of pneumatic drills erupted just outside my window. The noise was truly awful. It sounded something like a combination of a group of Flamenco dancers practicing too long and too hard, the worst experience one could have under a loud dentist drill, and the U.S. armored cavalry on carpet bombing maneuvers. Actually, it was the New York Telephone Company, eager to provide better service.

*After the first volley, my patient who had metaphorically levitated some three inches off the couch, turns his head toward me and says, "Did you get that." I say, "Sure did." He says with a slight giggle, 'If I had a hand grenade, I'd throw it at them, do you think it would take one or two to get them all?" I respond, "I think two would do just fine." He says, "Blow 'em up to bits, serve them right to fuck around us!" I respond, "Maimed beyond recognition!" He laughs, "Zap them we'll both get them, serves them right for disrupting my life." We go on like this, playing for a short time, sharing fantasies about what we could do to the "disrupters." **The patient is now frolicking in sadistic aggressive fantasies.** After a period of this, and the somewhat diminished objective barrage, my patient pauses and enters a lengthy silence. I say nothing. Tears roll down his cheeks, and* *he says, "That felt so good!" I thought for sure you would say I'm crazy or ask me why I came up with "hand grenade." "You just responded to me. I'm crying because my dad could never do that. He wouldn't let things go crazy. He would meekly reproach and tell me not to make problems, not to curse. We were playing? We were playing! I was playing, and you were playing too! You didn't take me seriously, did you? (I did, but not the meta-communication. Only the content and transference meanings.) "God, I wish he had the character to do that. It's such a freedom. This is overwhelming. It was so funny! So, I'm sadistic, big deal, it's a fantasy. I have a right to express it and feel it. So does my passion. I am not my father! Jesus... I've got to get tenure. I can make waves (recalling his father's admonition "to not make waves.") I'm so damned up, as if I had no right to ambition, to kill someone off. Wait, it won't knock my dad off if I have ambition. I'll just do what he couldn't do. I do want to be a professor, etc."*

At the moment we engaged in our repartee, I believe we were in a full-fledged "playing alliance." **We were creating a scene that fit the moment and had curative qualities.** *The experience was timeless (in the moment), it was a secure mutually affective state, and I was free enough to be a responsive audience to my patient's play (which called for free play in the service of a therapeutic resolution) rather than be a critic of its manifestation or an interpreter of its content. My comprehension and personal repertoire of ways of being enabled for what the scene required, I was capable of staying with the emergent transference testing experience, rather than make a transference interpretation of what he was trying to induce in me. I call this way of consciously being with the patient an*

91

"Actment" that required both judgment on my part as well as a capacity to play in the moment in the service of a sense of what was needed, without my feeling threatened by entering into such an experience. This is a process different from an enactment which is an unconscious acting out with the patient. Of course, the play was one thing, while the humor in the situation masked the aggressive, competitive, and, may I say, murderous feelings toward me which were eventually to emerge as part of the transference within our working alliance and relationship.

Assistant Prof. L. was well on his way to becoming Associate Professor – in more ways than one.

The above vignette, I believe, illustrates the importance of understanding the *context* of a given therapeutic moment as it emerges, rather than prematurely interpreting the content of the material. If I reflect back on the way I handled the situation in the split seconds in which it emerged, I can in linear form attempt to explain the combination of subjective and objective dimensions which enabled my intervention. All occurring in a layered *instance* based on my knowledge of my patient's idiosyncratic history, my sensing the context, and my available repertoire of ways of being. Although we had an effective working relationship up to that point, my patient and I were very separate entities with clear and discrepant roles. He was the patient and I was the therapist; cognitive understanding and interpretations of transferential material were comprehended in the rational and collaborative mind of the patient. But what seemed to have been missing was any deeply expressed affective involvement between us. We had worked well together, but had never "played." When the terribly intrusive and external drilling noise impinged into our session, we had a mutual and unifying reaction to it. When Assistant Professor L. said, "Did you get that?" my internal associations went to "Did I get the disturbance?" Then, "Did his father get the noise he (my patient) wanted to make? Then to the noise, he, my son, needed me to encourage him to make. Then to my feeling about noisy intrusion, which seemed aggressive to me no, hostile, then for the moment I was envious of those people (workers) able to make noise without considering other's needs. No, but the workers were doing their job. Did I just want to ignore it, and stay with the content of the session? I imagined myself as his father. That's what he might do! The newspaper story flashed in in my mind. What was my patient communicating? I thought he might be displacing his anger, or was he wishing for me to help him bring his anger into the session? I thought of Melanie Klein, was he ready to integrate a split? I thought of his Oedipal father. I thought of the noise emanating from his parents' bedroom he once alluded to hearing. Competitive feelings with me? I went over my palette of theories… Did he need me to be a self-object? What had been going on in the previous session? What had he just been saying before he asked, "Did you get that?" Oh yes! The newspaper route story, another example of his father not encouraging his aggression, his ambition… I remained an involved audience to him… merely saying, "Sure did." I let myself be organized by what he would respond to next. Which was, with a slight giggle, "If I had a hand grenade…" He was feeling aggressive, hostile, why not? I sensed his need for my response. Would I be with him? Not just an interpretation of his developing aggression but an affective validation of its quality. I was, and we were in the playframe and I did not want to allude to it and ruin the affective moment… Unlike Charlie Chaplin's audience,

I was not driven away or merely reacting to the seriousness of the message (the patient's shadow), but rather to its meta-source. This approach paved the way for an open and more affectively meaningful working relationship. The freedom experienced within the playing alliance would remain a solid understructure, enabling and abetting subsequent deeper qualities to the working relationship (alliance) as the treatment continued.

Knowing what the particular moment calls for, and awareness of the playing versus working alliance concept I have elucidated, helped me organize the sessions and help the patient in a way that was most constructive for his development at the moment. Of course, this traded on our mutual capacity to play, as an option in terms of the context in the session. We never lost the frame, rather we expanded it.[23] I was an empathic involved audience to his message and vice versa.

The Continuum of Play and Serious Levels of Relating: an Example from Group Therapy

One of the things that makes us" more human than otherwise" is our ability to relate to ourselves and others at different levels of experience and understanding. The ability to play, share humor, experience anger, take someone seriously, and empathically be involved are just some of these different levels which are crucial to our being fully in this world and in potential connection with others. I believe what organizes our therapeutic comprehension of various group levels is our ability to use our judgment sufficiently to enter into what the momentary context is, or ought to be

---

23 This is an important notion, as I like to think of "expanding the box" as opposed to going "out of the box."

about. Confusion about this, on the part of the therapist, often changes the trajectory of where a relationship or group experience is going. I will now discuss some of my ideas and experiences on this theme, as I currently shape them as a group therapist.

The Group Therapist as an "Experiencer" and Organizer of the Group Montage: An Analogy from Film

The group therapist is involved with both experiencing how the group is organizing itself through the process of developing its own momentary scenes, and, perhaps like a film director, selects which scenes to emphasize. Continuity may be present or it may not be, depending on what level the therapist understands what is happening. Someone reports a dream. It may mean something about an underlying factor in the group or it may be experienced as an intrusion, or welcome stimulant, or still again its content may evoke another member's affective response or a historical personal memory, etc. What to say, or in fact whether to say anything and, most importantly, when to say something, depends upon the therapist's judgment and comfort with the paradox of experience and observation. Similar to montage in a film, the group therapist is involved through his interventions in what is to be emphasized during the continuous stream of group process.

Literality versus Play in the Individual and Group Situation: The Example of Rupert: "The buck stops here!"

One of Rupert's favorite expressions was, "if you play now, you'll pay later." An only child, Rupert had been brought up in a highly rule-regulated environment by irrational and explosive parents. They fought between themselves and with Rupert. He lived in a world of sadistic aggression and had inhibited his sexual interests until he was in his early twenties. Now in his late forties, he came to my group with the hope of working on his interpersonal behavior and desire/capacity to find a mate he could be "serious with." Rupert had numerous girlfriends and had been engaged twice, and twice had broken the engagement. He labeled himself as "not a very promising catch." He knew he was cynical and mistrusting and his humor, though available, was sarcastic. In the group he was surprised to be accepted by most of the members, (even those he tried to alienate seemed to accept him) and slowly, though not so surely, Rupert increasingly felt safer and somewhat vulnerable as he moved into his third year of group therapy.

The session I am using as an example occurred in the middle of his third year. He had been discussing difficulties he had with his current girlfriend who he described as unduly resentful because he asked her to sleep over on a Saturday night, only to have her leave the next day so he could watch a football game on television alone. He had had "enough" of her and it was "time for her to go." Although it was a serious dynamic, Rupert presented it with his usual cynical humor saying, "I know this will not make me popular with the women in this group." In response, there was some knowing laughter, as one female patient, Selma, drawing on her own positive domestic experience, wondered why Rupert could not have simply watched the game with his girlfriend present as she did with her husband. They could be in each other's company, be at leisure, and enjoy a "different kind of moment," she suggested. Rupert's response was, "Well, *then she might really think I am serious with her, and that I might actually enjoy her company when not having a real reason to, like sex."*

In response, someone else in the group said, *"This is what you do here, you want what you want when you want it, but if not, you just can't "be" with us."* Soon after, Selma, a carefree female patient, said she would like to throw one of the couch pillows at him *"to loosen him up, because he was so uptight."* Rupert, visibly angry, responded with *"Don't you dare!"* George, a playful man, then says to Selma, *"Well, throw it to me, I'll play."* Selma did just that, and George threw the pillow back at her playfully. Selma, then threw it to Bill, and Bill threw it to Lois, Lois threw it to Mary and, Mary, hesitatingly but with gusto, threw it to me, and then I threw it to Selma. Everyone was laughing. Selma then tossed it to Rupert. He held the pillow tightly and said, *"The buck stops here, let's get serious."* Members of the group responded with the belief that this was exactly the problem. When asked what he was experiencing when the pillow came to him, Rupert reflected angrily that what was seen as play, with a message attached about allowing himself to be freely involved with the group, was taken literally by Rupert as a form of inappropriate group behavior. Further, he experienced it as an indicator of aggression and avoidance and did not entirely see the humor in the play as well as an attempt to playfully "reach" him. It might be said that Rupert went with a literal analysis of the event based upon his subjective belief concerning what was serious, rather than the experience of the moment and its metaphoric implications.[24] His literality got in the way of the spontaneity

---

24 Among other things, the pillow represented a condensation of both the women he "tossed away" as well as "a woman's" (Selma's) desire to reach him playfully," etc.

enacted. The group members eventually did empathize, rather than criticize him for his subjective experience. This helped pave the way for his further reflection on the issue. As the group therapist I would have stepped in, if the group had been solely severely and unreflectively critical of his "stopping the action" and thus making him into a "bad object."

I trust that this example illustrates how the inhibition of nonverbal spontaneous enactments can stop, spoil, or prevent the experience of play to happen. Like the analyst who is too quick to search for the underlying meaning of a behavior and sometimes as a result misses the significant moment of an experience: (in this case an intimate playfulness, which was also a nonverbal message, since verbal messages seemed to go nowhere at the moment) some patients too search for meaning as a defense against experience. To me, the group was bringing Rupert a message in a playful way and encouraging him to take part in being in a play space without making verbal interpretations of his actions. Rupert's experience of "stopping the action" was subsequently valuable to interpret, based on the immediate experience we (almost) all shared. As the therapist, my entry into this play moment was a conscious *actment* as opposed to an unconscious *enactment*.

What I Saw as the Analyst:

Returning to the example of Rupert. What happened? First of all, the group moved into a playful *and* defensive posture through the humor involved in tossing the pillow around. I, as the analyst, could have stopped the action at this point and interpreted or inquired about the underlying meaning, thereby changing the group montage. I could have verbally interpreted Selma's attempt to "reach " Rupert," etc. and/or perhaps there was Oedipal Jealousy, (Selma has feelings for Rupert, who reminds her of her father). Then there was George competing with Rupert for Selma ("Throw the pillow to me," he says) as well as George's narcissistic need for attention getting, and displaying a sexuality in the service of warding off unconscious feelings of impotency (he had gone through a series of urinary tract infections), regressive behavior (tossing pillows) as a defense against dealing with issues verbally (acting in). Rupert's fear of women in the group, his fear of the group getting out of control, and misreading of spontaneous play as a frozen equivalent to his parents fighting. Therefore needing to "stop it." The wish to re-enact being a scapegoat, etc. Instead, I chose to let the process unfold, without fearing it would get out of control. How it was stopped was as significant as how it started. The group had became a safe playground to enact a set of feelings which could later be reflected upon by each individual… A play space that might have been viewed by a different group leader as an avoidance of work in the group, and prematurely curtailing the "work" of play.

In fact, the expression of free play and humor set the pace for later reflection by each member, which I believe would *not* have been so effectively worked on if it had it been prematurely curtailed. I am happy to say that over time, even for Rupert, so encapsulated in his way, did indeed get a dollop of salubrious interpersonal experience out of this and various other group interactions that helped soften a rather rigid crust hiding a softer personality.

A Further Note on the Working Alliance and an Attempted Playful Communication When It Occurs at the Wrong Time

Paul, a tall lanky middle-aged historian who had left academia to work in business, had come into treatment due to a sense of woodenness, and difficulty in his second marriage. Though a good father, he was emotionally distant with his wife who he felt "bossed him around." He was also quite distant in general. Pushed into therapy by his wife, it took some time to develop a minimal working relationship.

When I first met him, Paul seemed to have virtually no sense of an internal life. For example, he recalled no dreams, and it took us a long time to engage in the process of an analytically oriented therapy. Affective interchange was not a significant part of his childhood and adolescent family experience, which was one of the reasons he was in group therapy as well as individual treatment. His father, a military man who had one arm severed in a training accident, had died suddenly when Paul was thirteen. The vignette I am describing below occurred in the middle stages of our work. Having missed two previous group sessions due to a business trip overseas, Paul was unusually buoyant in this group. Usually reticent, and tending to reveal things about himself only when asked, Paul involved himself in this group experience early. There had been a conflict in the group between Wilma and Klaus the week before and it was continuing to be dealt with in this session. Paul, who had not been present the week before, began to unself-consciously, enthusiastically, and somewhat intrusively explain what had happened! Clearly it was his way of trying to fit in, as awkward as it was, but when asked by various group members, who responded with surprise but not really critically, to his facile hypothesizing, Paul denied he was being facile, reiterating, "He just knew he was right." My own intervention in the face of his remarks was un-empathic and counter-transferential. (I thought I was playfully giving him a paradoxical message about making conclusions without direct experience of a situation – specifically by including myself in such a process.) I said, "*This can be a problem with some historians as well as some analysts who are making conclusions. When you weren't even there and you have a theory.*" I thought I was making it easier for him to hear by joining him and poking fun at myself as well! Paul's immediate response was to laugh. Some members laughed at both Paul and me (no one picked up on the latent competition I later felt was going on, i.e., Paul too could make interventions). The group went on, with the issue between Klaus and Wilma, with minimal discussion of Paul's construction. As the group progressed, Paul began to withdraw, and I felt internally upset that I might have put a damper on his enthusiasm. I sensed that he had organized his experience of me as a message to "shut up," rather than a playful intervention that would help him reflect.

My internal thoughts about my impact on him persisted. I sensed that he must be hurt, and angry at me, but could not say it or perhaps not even feel it internally. Had our tenuous alliance broken down by my moving too quickly into what I thought was a play mode as a way of avoiding some other issue of mine!? I said nothing. A short time went by and Paul impulsively blurted out a flurry of somewhat unwarranted anger at Wilma for her past insensitivity in dealing with Klaus in the group. To me this sounded like displacement, and I shared my subjective thought that perhaps Paul was having feelings towards Wilma which contained emotions he felt towards me and my supposed playful comment. Specifically, I said, "I was wondering how you experienced my comment about historians to you earlier in the session. I feel badly about it because I experienced you as full of enthusiasm, and instead of saying that, (or restating my full intervention with that) I focused on how could you understand something that occurred when you were not present, so I'm thinking about how you experienced my comment and if you are angry at me for the way I made it?"

Paul seemed to be taken aback, but felt my specificity helped him be clear about his experience. He acknowledged that he did feel upset, but thought – "*Oh, just let it be…It was only a momentary feeling, and you were right anyway.*" I then responded by saying, even though I may have been right, I unwittingly became another authority figure (like his mother) telling him what to do and not do, likely shaming him, and missed letting him know that I appreciated his enthusiasm, under the misguided guise of trying to be humorous by including both of us in my intervention. Paul was visibly moved, saying "*I never expected an acknowledgement from you in the group. I feel surprised, I guess I hold a different picture of you about the way you can be.*" Here I was also fortunate that other members of the group could say that I was flexible and not rigid and could, like anyone else, make "mistakes." Paul then shared a series of associations and a flood of memories about the years he lived in a northwestern city during his youth, a time he never had previously mentioned and had himself virtually repressed. His first ten years were in this working-class community. It was a tough time, but also a warm time, with a warm "whole" father. Soon after his father severed his arm, the family moved to a southwestern town and an environment which emphasized his mother's religion. His father was a Catholic and had disagreements with his mother as a Protestant about which church to attend. In the northwestern city, Paul had been happily involved with his father's church activities, but when they moved to the southwest, he attended somewhat forcibly his mother's Protestant church, while his father stayed home not joining them in the services.

So what Happened?

My countertransference response initially inhibited a somewhat brittle working relationship. My recovery – based on what I sensed was a displacement of feelings towards me onto Wilma and my validation of this displacement through my inquiry into Paul's experience – buttressed my expressing to Paul and the rest of the group how I organized my experience and enabled the ongoing development of the working relationship. In effect, I had momentarily lost being an *involved audience* for Paul and entered into a premature and awkward attempt at a humorous playing alliance as a way of not dealing with his enthusiasm on one level and his competitiveness with me or mine with his, on another. I tried to play, where I should have worked by acknowledging his enthusiasm, rather than solely focus on the content of his message. As a result of this interchange, Paul, in both individual and group sessions:

1. Continued to work with his experience of me as previously repressed affect-laden material emerged.
2. My humanness in the "real relationship" demonstrated my comfort with him and my wish to truly understand him and need for him to express his experience of my impact on him. (Unlike his mother who wanted

him more involved with her religion, rather his comfort with his father's – partly a reality of his experience of me in that moment on his part.)

3. This paved the way for me to more deeply understand and encourage Paul's capacity to express his feeling state in the moment, to relate more directly in the here and now.

Eventually the context of warmth paved the way for Paul's recollection of conflicted, angry, and competitive feelings towards female peers and older women, as well as dealing with an underlying depression based on the loss of a father he had not fully mourned. From my perspective, this illustrates the analyst's need to be comfortable with both objective reality and subjective experience. The former is illustrated by my displacement hypothesis, my awareness of latent competition (both his and mine), and what I initially understood as manic defense (overly enthusiastic after missing two groups) rather than an urgent desire, even if misguided, to belong, and demonstrate he was involved, even when he was away; my empathic inquiry to his reaction to my intervention as well as my self-disclosure of sharing my feeling about how I felt, successfully rectified the mis-attunement.[25] The above example illustrates the prematurely narrowing and subsequent recovery of the scope and divergent quality of my internal associations, thereby enabling a more empathic sense of the patient's self and our mutual dynamic at that moment. By prematurely putting one theory too early into the foreground, instead of freely playing with my internal associations, I almost foreclosed the affective

---

25 My disclosure was "field-relevant" (Brok 1985) which means an analyst's self-disclosure of an internal state relevant to the current situation. "Field- relevant self-disclosure is a disclosure of one's personal dynamics or genetic content. It is not to be used except in highly unique and special circumstances.

involvement and validation of my patient's experience which was needed to promote a more meaningful basis for our therapeutic work. I could have easily and inadvertently promoted a false self-perpetuation in Paul. My recovery, and the way I chose to use it, I believe, enabled me to a once again become a receptive audience to my patient's enthusiastic "being" with the group in a way that was awkward in content but well-meant in connection via his uncharacteristic enthusiastic attitude. This at the moment was more important than becoming enmeshed in his shadow by prematurely (for him) focusing on the objective derivatives of his subjective experience. Acceptance of the paradoxical fact that all my potential interventions were accurate, but only one was most relevant given where the patient was located, and an important clinical observation that singular theory driven approaches (including intersubjective) must inevitably yield to the context. We simply need to attend to the context of any moment in therapy from within a broad developmental -ecological framework and choose based upon where the patient is located in that framework. Recognition of Paul's playful enthusiasm is an example of one such moment, and how my choice was eventually made. I became a more involved audience" with recognition of where the patient was "at." This is an example of what I have termed the "playing alliance" and is, I trust, one useful route to making a growth-promoting therapeutic intervention.

CHAPTER 7

What Can We Learn from Charlie?

As we followed Chaplin's film career in this monograph, we can see that his attempt to integrate play, seriousness, humor, and reality was not always successful, as he lost a significant portion of his audience that just found it distasteful or too incongruous with their own real life experiences or political situations that were *just not funny*, or spoke to those in his audience who had either been traumatized or knew of others via family ties or identification who had been.

In retrospect, it is easy to laugh at some of his comedy, in the sense that it releases tension from fear of people such as Hitler or helps one rise above the fear to a sense of power. Viewing Hitler as a comic figure is one way of coping with the angst and fear that his being and politics evoked. We can think of Mel Brooks's successful film which features the song "Springtime for Hitler in Germany." Many of us laughed with delight at the parody, some twenty years after World War II, especially if we were not personally or directly affected by the Holocaust. However, I can recall an uneasy feeling in my reaction to this film about my own apparent "triumph of humor" over very terrifying experiences that many people, including my own relatives, had undergone as Holocaust survivors, and of those who had perished. The same with *Life is Beautiful*, the 1998 award-winning film by Robert Benigni. as well as the current 2019 film *Jojo Rabbit*, directed by Wake Taititi, which won the audience award at the Toronto International Film Festival (Sept 2019). As one reviewer aptly put it:

The question of how much and what kind of fun is permissible to have with Nazis never goes away, and the resurgence of right-wing extremism around the world makes the question newly uncomfortable. When Jojo Rabbit, *showed up at the Toronto International film Festival in September, the fact that it played Hitler at least partly for laughs – with the director Taika Waititi impersonating a goofy, gangly almost lovable Fuhrer, you could hear the wincing from across the border. The relative innocuousness of the film doesn't entirely dispel the uneasiness around it. A.O. Scott,* New York Times, *Oct 20, 2019, p. 10.*

For *The Great Dictator*, it was quite difficult to view for many in the moment and, indeed, for years after for those who went through the Holocaust or who knew people personally or about people murdered in the camps. There is a limit to laughing at tragedy, and our capacity for denial can become pathological to the extent that we rely on not feeling upset when watching someone make fun of someone who killed people in one's family, or anyone for that matter. The same goes for the theme of *Monsieur Verdoux*, where humor/play is attempted to be interjected into the murder of innocent women, double dealing and taking advantage for the benefit of the protagonist's family, or using nuclear bombing where millions are killed as an exculpatory rationale. And so it goes, humor and play can be a great way of relating and loosening up rigidities, but can also be an escape from fear and unconsciously recalled traumas.

My counter-transferential and misguided attempt to play with Paul about being knowledgeable about something he did not experience is a mild example of this. On the other hand, my comfort with playing with my patient Professor L. was a wonderful, validating developmental experience for him and a satisfying, therapeutic creative joy for me, while allowing and participating in a play space rather than too quickly intervening and interpreting. What happened in the group with Rupert is a good example of being able to play and not feel shame or guilt about being involved in that manner when the context called for it therapeutically.

In a situation where the context is comfortable, the paradox of play/humor with seriousness/reality can be salubrious. Where the context is such that one of the witnesses to the experience has a history of trauma, and pain, the paradoxical pairing of play/ humor with reality/seriousness has significant limitations.

References

Allison,E. & Campbell, C., (2019). Commentary on "Trust comes from a sense of feeling one's self in Sarah Schoen, Afraid to Commit: Proposing Psychoanalysis and the Paradox of the Analyst's Desire, *Contemporary Psychoanalysis*, 51:4, 649–679.

Anderegg, D. (1989) Playing in developmental psychology and in psychoanalytic theory, *Psychoanalysis and Contemporary Thought*, 12, #4, 535–563.

Auerhann, N. C. & Laub, D, (1987) Play and playfulness in Holocaust Survivors. *Psychoanalytic Study of the Child*, 42. 45–58.

Balint, M. (1968) *The Basic Fault*, Evanston, Ill Northwestern Univ.

Baranger, W. & Baranger, M (1962) The analytic situation as a dynamic field, *International Journal of psychoanalysis 89: 795-826.*

Bach, S., (2019). States of Self Surrender, *Psychoanalytic Psychology* , 39:2 159–165.

Barker, R.G, (1968) *Ecological Psychology*, Stanford Univ. Press.

Bateson, G. (1972) A theory of Play and Fantasy, in *Steps to an Ecology of the Mind*, New York, Ballantine Books, 177–193.

Black Swan, (2010) Film. Darren Aronofsky, Director.

Brok, A. J. (1982) Furthering the working alliance with the more difficult patient. *Paper presented at American Psychological Association*, Washington , DC.

Brok, A. J. (1985) Field Relevant self disclosure, Concept developed for course In Group Therapy, *Training Institute for Mental Health and Postgraduate Center for Mental Health*, NY.

Brok, A. J. (1991a) The experience of play and joy in psychotherapy and psychoanalysis. Invited Address, *Oklahoma Society for Psychoanalytic Studies, Local Chapter of Division 39 (Psychoanalysis), American Psychological Assoc.* (Sept 7).

Brok, A. J. (1991b) The playing alliance in film and on the couch. *Invited Presentation, Eleventh annual Spring Meeting, Div. 39 (Psychoanalysis), American Psychoogical Assoc.*, Chicago, Ill.

Brok, A. J. (1992, February). What if Freud had been a Group Therapist? *Invited presentation: 50th anniversary of the American Group Psychotherapy Association.* New York, N.Y.

Brok, A.J. (2003) Hope, illusion and reality in analytic group therapy, *Invited presentation, Spring meeting, Div 39 (Psychoanalysis) American Psychological .* Assoc. Minneapolis, MN.

Brok, A. J. (2004). Couple dynamics, group dynamics, general dynamics? *Group, 28,* 143–156.

Brok, A. J. (2005) Father and daughter: Historical Identification, Present Attachments, Trauma, and the question of Passionate involvement: *American Journal of Psychoanalysis,* vol 65 (1) March, 2005, 53–69.

Brok, A. J. (2006) What can an analyst learn from Charlie Chaplin? *Invited presentation, annual Spring meeting, Div 39 (Psychoanalysis) American Psychological Assoc.* New Orleans, LA .(Aug. 10).

Brok, A. J. (2008) God sometimes plays dice with the universe. *Invited Presentation: Spring Meeting, Div. 39 (Psychoanalysis) American Psychological Assoc.*, New York. N.Y.

Brok, A. J. (2013) Montage in cinema and the analytic session, invited presentation *First congress on Cineanalisis, INCAA & Argentine psychoanalytic association Sept 12, 2013. Buenos Aires, Argentina.*

Brok, A. J. (2014). El Montaje en el cine y en la session analitica , UBA, Buenos Aires, *Etica y Cine,* Vol 4 # 2, pp 63–70.

Brok, A. J. (2015). The importance of montage in analytic therapy: Experience in Argentina and the United States. Introductory remarks, First USA Congress on *Psychoanalysis and Film; Connections, Synergies and Differences Perspectives from Latin America and the United States* Conference sponsored by Diversity Committee of the Institute for Psychoanl. Training and Research., Dept of Clinical Psychology, New School for Soc. Research;. Association for Psychoanal. Medicine, the Collaborating Assoc. of the Columbia Univ. Center for Training ; Section 1 of the Div. of Psychoanalysis of the APA and the Training Institute For Mental Health, NY. *New School for Social Research, NY. July 18.*

Brok, A. J. (2016) A look at levels in Relating in Group Therapy*: Group,* 40 (4), 303–312. *Buenos Aires Herald,* (1940) Dec 28, pages 1 and 4.

Chaplin, C (1964) *My Autobiography,* Simon and Schuster, NY

Chaplin, C (1921). *The Kid,* Key Video Version, 1989

Chaplin, C (1925) *The Gold Rush,* Key Video Version, 1989.

Chaplin, C. (1931) *City Lights,* Key Video Version, 1989

Chaplin, C. (1936). *Modern Times,* Key Video Version, (1989)

Chaplin, C (1940). *The Great Dictator,* Key Video Version. (1989)

Chaplin, C (1947). *Monsieur Verdoux*. Key Video Version (1989)

Chaplin, C (1952). *Limelight* Key Video Version (1989)

Chaplin, C. (1957). *A King in New York*, Key Video Version (1989)

Clark, R. (1971) *Einstein, the life and times*, New York, Avon.

Chasseguet-Smirgel, J. (1985) *The Ego Ideal.* New York, W.W. Norton.

Chasseguet-Smirgel (1988) The triumph of humor, in H.P. Blum, Y. Kramer, A.K. Richards, & A. D. Richards, Edts: *Fantasy, myth and reality*: Essays in honor of Jacob Arlow, Madison, Ct, Inter. Univ. Press (197-213).

Crowther, B, in *New York Times* (1992) March 22, Pagers 11 and 16.

Duscinski, R., Collver, J & Carel, H (2019), Trust comes from a sense of feeling one's self understood by another mind. : An interview with Peter Fonagy. *Psychoanalytic Psychology*. 36:3 224–227.

Ehrenberg, D.E. (1990), Playfulness in the psychoanalytic relationship/*Contemporary Psychoanalysis l,* vol. 26 (1), pp. 74–95.

Freud, S. (1927) *Humor*: SE. XXI, London, Hogarth Press: 159–166.

Fromm, M.G. (1989). Winnicott's work in relation to classical psychoanalysis and ego psychology in M.G. Fromm and L. Smith (Eds.), *The facilitating environment, clinical applications of Winnicott's theory* , International Universities Press, Madison, CT.: 3–26.

Haining, P (1983*) The legend of Charlie Chaplin*, W.H. Allen, London. 106–107.

Irving, K (2019) The role of humor in priming intersubjectivity, *Psychoanalytic Psychology* 36,3 :207 – 215.

James, W. (1890_ *The principles of psychology*, 1, New York, Dover (1950).

Kerr, W. (1971) in *Focus on Chaplin*, Editor, Donald McCafferey, p. 148 Prentice Hall, Englewood -Cliff. New Jersey.

Life is Beautiful (1997). Film, Robert Benigni, Director.

Lewin, K. (1943) Defining the field at a given time, in D. Cartwright. Ed.. *Field theory in social science.* New York, Harper: 43–59.

Lynn, K (1997). *Charlie Chaplin and his times,.* NY Simon and Shuster.

Milton, J. (1996), *Tramp: the life of Charlie Chaplin,* . NY Harper Collins

Mitchell, S. (1991) The therapeutic situation as paradoxical experience, *Psychoanalytic Dialogues,* 1: 13–28.

Modell, A.M. (1990) *Other times, other realities.* Cambridge, Mass. Harvard Univ. Press: 55.

Modell, A. M. (1993). *The private self, Boston, Mass.* Harvard Univ. Press.

Modell, A. M. (2003) *Imagination and the meaningful brain,* Cambridge, MIT Press.

New York Times (2019) October 24. Google Claims Computing Feat Akin to 1st Flight. Section A, Page 1 of the New York edition

Ogden, T H.. (1989). Playing, dreaming and interpreting experience: comments on potential space. In M.G. Fromm , and B.L. Smith, eds. *Clinical Applications of Winnicott's theory.* Madison, CT. International Universities Press: 255–278.

Pasquali, G. (1987) Some notes on humour in psychoanalysis. *International review of psychoanalysis. 14 (2): 231–236.*

Pizer,, S.A (1992) The negotiation of paradox in the analytic process *Psychoanalytic Dialogues,* 02, Nov.: 215–240.

Reading, R.A., Safran, JD., Origlieri, A, & Murran, J. Christopher, (2019) Investigating Therapeutic reflective functioning. Therapeutic process and outcome, understood by another mind." *Psychoanalytic Psychology,* 36:2 :115–121,

Robinson, D. (1985). *Chaplin his life and art.* New York, Mc Graw-Hill.

Sandler, J.& Sandler, A 1978). On the development of object relationships and Affects. *International Journal of Psycho-Analysis.* 59: 285–296.

Schoggen, P, (1989) *Behavior Settings: a revision and extension of the work of Roger G. Barker's Ecological Psychology*, Stanford Univ. Press.

Stolorow and Atwood (1992) *Contexts of being.* New Jersey, Analytic Press.

Weiner, Brok and Snadowsky (1974) *Working with the Aged*, Prerntice Hall, NY.

Weissman, S. (2008) *Chaplin, A Life*, NY Arcade: 3-4, 45, 53, 71, 78, 255, 263.

Winnicott, D. W. (1971) *Playing and reality*, New York, Basic Books.

Yerushalmi, H. (1992). On the concealment of the interpersonal therapeutic reality in the course of supervision. *Psychotherapy: Theory, Research, Practice, Training*, 29 (3): 438–446.

www.ingramcontent.com/pod-product-compliance
Lightning Source LLC
Chambersburg PA
CBHW051247020426

42333CB00025B/3090